Cherokee Wisdom
12 Lessons to Becoming a Powerful Leader

2nd Edition
Timeless Native Wisdom

Cynthia M Ruiz & Abraham Bearpaw

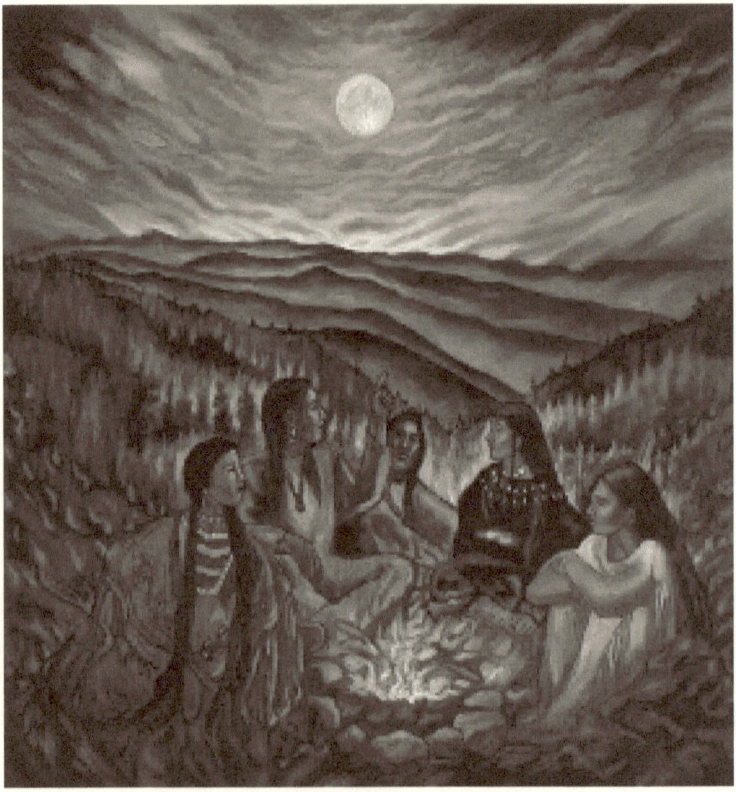

Cherokee Wisdom

"As the leader of the Cherokee people, it comes with great responsibility, but great opportunities to help my people grow stronger and go further."

Chuck Hoskin Jr
Principal Chief Cherokee Nation
6/1/19 to present

ISBN-13 9798652736972

Cherokee Wisdom

Welcome To The 2nd Edition!

Since the book was first published, I have been amazed at the great response which was received. I have participated in over 75 radio shows and Podcast all over the world. Many people have expressed interest in the teachings of our people. I certainly do not take credit for this knowledge as it has been passed down by my ancestors.

The Cherokee way is to strive for harmony and balance. That is why in this second edition I have invited Abraham Bearpaw to give his unique perspective as a Cherokee man. A man that has stayed strong during his life struggles to become a great leader. No one has a perfect life and for me, the quality of a great leader is someone who faces challenges and uses them as lessons.

I had the great pleasure of meeting Abraham Bearpaw, who has now become a good friend. His aunt Wilma Mankiller was the only female Principal Chief of the Cherokee Nation. Although I never had the pleasure of meeting her, my Mother would speak of her often.

Cherokee Wisdom

Abraham and I have had the opportunity to collaborate on several events in the Southern California area. He has always been responsible, hard-working and has shown a desire to continue the traditional ways of our Cherokee Ancestors. His Cherokee name is Bear (yona). I like to call him Brother Bear. I am so happy he has stepped up to the challenge and agreed to partner with me on the 2nd edition of this book. His unique perspective adds value and I know he comes from a place of integrity.

Leadership is a topic that is being talked about in many circles. In this complicated world taking a look back at our ancestors' ways is very important. As discussed in the book, as Cherokee leaders we take into consideration 7 generations before us and 7 generations into the future when making decisions.

I believe that if all leaders took this perspective the world would be a different place and we would not have the climate crisis and unnecessary violence we face today.

My journey has continued and I continue to evolve as a leader and a woman. In 2019 I was very humbled to receive the Cherokee Nation Community Leader of the year award. I do not see this a reflection of me but rather the work I have built on by the amazing Cherokee women in my family. My Grandmother, my Mother, and my Aunts.

In early 2020 I received my Cherokee name. During a ceremony with a Cherokee Elder, I was given the name "Lion Mother" (tluh-da-ji eh-ji). This name symbolizes a person who is a protector, teacher, and advisor. Someone who watches over the people and takes action for the good of the people. I strive to live up to the responsibility of my Cherokee name. I would like to express gratitude to Earnie L. Frost for being the vehicle to deliver my name

We ask that you be a part of the conversation and discuss these concepts with the people around you. Help us share this information because it does not belong to us, it belongs to the world.

Cynthia M Ruiz
Lion Mother

Cherokee Wisdom

Disclaimer

Although this book is based on Public information received from Cherokee Nation, we do not claim to represent or speak for the organization. The opinions in this book are our interpretations of the information and we recognize there are the elected officials which have the role of speaking in an official capacity. We have the utmost respect for Principal Chief Chuck Hoskin Jr and his administration. Cherokee Nation is a sovereign nation and we abide by all its rules and policies.

Acknowledgements

First and foremost, I must express gratitude to the Creator. The love and the divine presence of the Creator has brought me to this place where I can share this wisdom with you.

I would like to take this opportunity to express my love and gratitude to my amazing son Arturo D. Chavez and his wife Jacqueline. Special acknowledgement to my brother Jesse who is also my personal trainer and hiking buddy helping me stay healthy and grounded. My family's unconditional love and support have made me a better person.

Juan Solis created the beautiful artwork on the cover of the book. He is a Los Angeles-based artist who has a God-given talent. Thank you for capturing the essence of my vision.

To my Soul Sister Jeannie (Sister Weeping Willow), thanks for keeping me connected to the Universal Consciousness and the Creator.

This book is dedicated to all my ancestors who have come before me and who are now in the non-physical world. To my grandmother and Aunt

Sue, your presence is still felt. Thank you for the knowledge and wisdom you have bestowed on me — I am eternally grateful. I hope this information is helpful to others so we can create a generation of leaders that have the wisdom and compassion to make this planet a better place for the generations to come.

Acknowledgments from Abraham Bearpaw

I want to first give thanks to the Creator for the beautiful gift of life that we all receive and for the opportunity that we all have to make the world a better place. I also am thankful for my ancestors whose perseverance and sacrifice made it possible for our people to continue to exist and flourish. Also, though it seems like a lot; I want to acknowledge the following people who all in some way contributed to me being here and being able to turn my life around and help others.

I want to thank my parents, Vanessa Mankiller and Stan Bearpaw who were kind and supportive

Cherokee Wisdom

of me in all of my endeavors. They wanted only for my siblings and I to be happy and responsible.

I am grateful for my children who are amazing in spite of my drinking in their early years. Aidan, Colson, Vanessa, Aahlana and Trenton I am proud to be your Father. They are each perfect and I love them more than words can say. They inspire me every day to be a better man.

I also want to thank the mothers of my children who are all raising amazing humans and doing a fantastic job. Unfortunately, they did not get my best because of my substance use in the past but I am happy work to work together now as a team to support our children and guide them.

I want to acknowledge my aunts and uncles who all tried to guide me through my darkest times. Your words were not in vain. I appreciate your support and leadership and am doing my best to make you all proud. Also, my brothers and sisters who show me every day what it means to be strong. You are all the best people that I know and I am excited to see what we can achieve as a family.

I want to acknowledge Cynthia Ruiz who is a great friend and a great leader. Thank you for asking me to be a part of this project. I look forward to working together for a very long time. James Mankiller, Robert Friedman and John Aaron I appreciate your support during my tough years and the example that you set for what a man should be. I also want to acknowledge Tristana Bogan for pushing me to write and start my own business in spite of the risks. I thank you for inspiring me to be creative.

Lastly, I want to thank each of you who are reading this. You all inspire me to be better every day. I see you all on social media and other places showing tremendous leadership in these perilous times and I just want you all to know that your hard work is not unnoticed. Yes, there are a lot of bad things happening but there are more good things happening…because of you. So, let's see what else we can accomplish together.

Cherokee Wisdom

Words from Abraham Bearpaw

> *"The most fulfilled people are the ones who get up every morning and stand for something larger than themselves. They are the people who care about others, who will extend a helping hand to someone in need or will speak up about an injustice when they see it."*
>
> —Wilma Mankiller

This quote by my aunt Wilma Mankiller fully encapsulates what it means to be a leader. I believe that leaders should not only expect others to "do what I say" but also know that they will "do what you do". Leadership means that you set the example for others to follow.

Osiyo nigada (Hello everyone). My name is Abraham Bearpaw but my Cherokee name is Yona (Bear). My parents are Stan Bearpaw and Vanessa Mankiller and I am from Rocky Mountain, Oklahoma. I am very happy to share with you my experience with these 12 Lessons for Becoming a Powerful Leader in the hopes that they aid you in your endeavors.

Cherokee Wisdom

I am currently the Family Perseverance Manager for a Tribal TANF program in Southern California. I am also a motivational speaker and I teach classes about how to use the values in Native Culture to reduce risk factors for substance abuse, diabetes and suicide; while also promoting wellness. The goal of my efforts is for participants to be able to "Walk in Balance" and live a fulfilled life of wellness. I uphold my aunt Wilma as the benchmark for leadership because I believe that she, like Cynthia Ruiz, embodied all twelve attributes of leadership. She sought guidance and wisdom from her ancestors just as I strive to follow the example that she set for my generation. Now, it is our turn to teach the next generation about how the bedrock of our perseverance and strength is found in our Cherokee culture.

I was taught about all of these values that are based on our cultural teachings from when I was little. However, as I grew, I began to view these teachings as less important and became enamored with making money and making a name for myself. I was not happy with the person that I had become and began to abuse alcohol and drugs. In short, I

Cherokee Wisdom

became a very selfish person which goes against all of our values. Leadership roles in Cherokee Culture are based in community service and are defined by unselfish characteristics. Leaders must be prepared to do what is best for their people and also think about future generations when making decisions. Thankfully, later in life I was able to get sober and I began to follow our cultural teachings again. Now, I am ready to share with others how our cultural teachings give us everything we need to succeed and help others.

So, how do these 12 lessons based in Cherokee culture square with being a leader in the present? Whether you are the CEO of a Fortune 500 company or the Chief of the Cherokee Nation, if you apply these lessons then you are well on your way to success. However, like all things these values must be applied and we have to practice to become proficient. I am not perfect in my pursuits but I never give up and I work hard to be a better person. On any given day we get to choose how we feel and what we do. No matter our station in life we are all leaders and are capable of great things.

Abraham Bearpaw (Bear)

Cherokee Wisdom

Introduction from 1st Edition

Understanding our ancestors, our heritage and our culture can be valuable. I believe if we take the time to learn our lineage, it will give us perspective and help us understand where we come from; thus, making our lives more fulfilling today.

We each have the potential to be a great leader, whether it be at work, home, school, social settings or in life in general. Sometimes we are prepared for leadership roles but other times we are placed in them without guidance and have to learn by trial and error.

Throughout my career I have held many leadership positions from being in student government while in college, running my own business, managing an organization of 5,000 employees, being an executive at the largest port in the nation, serving as a commissioner for the City of Los Angeles and being a mom. I have received over fifty awards or accolades for my leadership abilities. It has not always been easy, but I have always found the inner strength to rise to the occasion.

Cherokee Wisdom

Instead, we can build on the collective knowledge of previous generations. In my life, I have used the wisdom from my ancestors as a guidepost. So, I humbly share this knowledge which has guided me along my path. This wisdom comes from my ancestors, the Cherokee people.

One key message to pass forward is strive for simplicity, harmony and balance in your life. If you look around, you will notice the universe operates in simple movements, it operates in cycles. Everything has a beginning, middle and end. Open your eyes and look around to behold Mother Nature—the Moon, the Sun and the Seasons going through their stages. The ocean waves too have a harmonic rhythm, and becoming aware of that rhythm can help you feel connected to the universal consciousness and provide a sense of certainty.

I come from blended cultures, my father Mexican-American and my mother Native American Cherokee. I consider it a blessing to have such powerful heritage and believe that I have the best of both worlds. In this book I share mostly what I have learned from my Native American heritage.

Cherokee Wisdom

In 1896, my maternal grandmother, Joanna Lowrey, was born in Oklahoma on Indian territory. She had no need for a formal birth certificate since she was born at home. She was first officially recognized when she was four years old at which time she was placed on the Cherokee Rolls (No. 5409). That record was also referred to as the Dawes Rolls. By 1902 the Dawes Rolls listed 41,798 citizens of the Cherokee Nation.

My family and I are also registered members of the Cherokee Nation of Oklahoma. The Cherokee Nation is headquartered in Tahlequah, Oklahoma and today we have 350,000 citizens.

Several years ago, my Aunt Sue did some research to trace our family tree. The information which was used as the genealogical foundation came from a document that was written in 1889 and later purchased by the Smithsonian Institution in 1899. The author of that document, Lucy L. Keys, also known as Wah-ne-nau-hi, wrote about the customs, traditions and superstitions of the Cherokee people. It also included the family tree of the Lowrey family from which I am a direct descendant.

Cherokee Wisdom

I was so excited to see my roots actually shown on paper. The first ancestor recorded in our family tree was the life of Oo-loo-tsa, who appears to have lived in the 1600's. George Lowrey was fourth generation—born circa 1770. He was the oldest of seven children and played a significant role in the tribe. His friends called him Ah- gee-hli, which in the Cherokee language means rising or aspiring. He was good friends with Sequoyah, one of the most celebrated Cherokees in history for his creation of a reading and writing system that advanced the literacy of his people. In 1791 George traveled to Washington D.C. to solicit payment for the annuity promised to the Cherokee Nation in the treaty of 1785.

The mission was successful and he was hailed as a leader and respected by his people. I would like to think that leadership is in my blood.

But even before I uncovered the knowledge in my family tree, I felt a connection to my ancestors through my love for Mother Nature. I am a full-on city girl, yet I feel so grounded when I spend time in the bosom of Mother Earth. I have always enjoyed hiking and still hike to this day. It is a perfect way to

Cherokee Wisdom

get exercise and at the same time enjoy the beauty and majesty of Mother Earth.

I also have an internal awareness that we must all do our part to help the planet. I remember one day doing an interview with a reporter and she asked me, "When did you become an environmentalist?" and I replied, "I am Cherokee, I was born an environmentalist." Somethings we are born knowing information that was passed down from our ancestors. Though sometimes we can forget pieces of it, we each have the ability to tap into that historic knowledge from our individual pasts.

The information that I share here was outlined as a part of the "2010 Report to the Cherokee People." A portion of that report reads:

"Each of us, whether a Cherokee Nation employee or citizen, is responsible to lead our Nation to achieve a vision of becoming a happy and healthy people. Our leadership influences and shapes the behavior of those around us and determines the outcomes we choose Leadership takes us from where we are, to where we want to be. These attributes describe our understanding of leadership necessary to achieve our designed purpose."

In that report the twelve attributes of leadership were identified as cultural values, qualities or characteristics. We are all leaders in our own lives so I share this information with you in the hopes that you can become the best leader you can be. I believe that everyone can benefit from this knowledge, as it is applicable across all cultures and religions. These concepts and thoughts were passed down from generation to generation. Many are very similar to other cultures though with slight differences.

Each culture teaches values to their people to help guide them. These values shape what the culture considers right and wrong. Some cultures derive their values from the bible while others from various faiths or social movements or philosophies. Most Native Americans derive their values from the teachings of our ancestors, through storytelling until a formal language was developed.

I am not, nor do I claim to be a spokesperson for the Cherokee Nation. The Cherokee Nation has elected representatives who speak in an official capacity and I defer to them to speak for tribe. I have written this book from my perspective, and this is what I believe to be the truth. My perspective is based on my life experiences, which have been especially influenced by my community, family, friends and growing up bi-culturally in Los Angeles

I am aware that not everyone will agree with my interpretation. That is okay because it is my truth and I share my understanding with the best of intentions.

The cultural attributes I share with you are in no particular order and each chapter can stand alone. Each attribute is equal and has individual significance. They are also very intertwined and connected to one other. Yes, they have individual significance but they are strongest when looked at holistically.

We can all learn from each other. And as you will see from these teachings, my native roots ask that we guide others so they can benefit from this knowledge too. I have decided to share this information with you in the hope that it will make your life better and that you will find the leader within yourself.

Cherokee Wisdom

I believe that by incorporating these 12 lessons into your life, you can become a powerful leader. We each have the power within us. How do we tap into that power? One of the turning points for me was learning the practice of meditation. Looking around I noticed that many of the people I respected and considered powerful had one thing in common, they all meditated.

At first, I didn't get it. How could you turn within, sit still, be quite and become more powerful? For several years I attempted to meditate by taking workshops, classes and practice sessions. I was fine for a few minutes until I found myself distracted by my thoughts.

It was not until I took a meditation class with Reverend Michael Bernard Beckwith spiritual leaders at the AGAPE International Spiritual Center located in Los Angeles that I was able to understand how to deal with those pesky thoughts.

Prior to his class, I would sit and attempt to meditate. But as I was sitting there, thoughts would enter my mind. The thoughts were usually about what I had to do after I meditated or my list of things to do for that day.

Cherokee Wisdom

While taking Reverend Michael's class, the lightbulb went on. He said don't resist the thoughts when they come; acknowledge them, then release them without giving them any attention. So, when I am sitting in mediation and hear the dog barking, I don't concentrate on the dog barking. I acknowledge the sound and release it and it floats away without disrupting my meditative practice.

I was then able to take my meditation to the next level by spending a week at Deepak Chopra's center in Carlsbad where we mediated for hours at a time. Deepak, with his soothing voice and profound wisdom, helped me maintain the space to allow my power to expand. We all are powerful and have access to the power at any time because the source is a universal consciousness which I call the Creator.

I want you to take away from this book the parts that will help you along your journey. There will be some principles that will resonate with you more than others. The vast majority of what is in this book is likely information you already know, but sometimes in life it is good to get a reminder or hear someone else's perspective.

Cherokee Wisdom

So, take the lessons with you as you travel through your life and realize that we are all spiritual beings having a human experience and that we change and evolve every day.

I have also shared quotes, which I have found helpful along my journey.

Find the leader within you,
Cynthia M Ruiz

Cherokee Wisdom

In Iroquois society, leaders are encouraged to remember seven generations in the past and consider seven generations in the future when making decisions that affect the people.

Wilma Mankiller
Principal Cherokee Nation
1985-1995

Cherokee Wisdom

My Connection To The Ancestors

Coming from blended cultures and living in an urban environment, my connection to my Native American ancestors' teachings have been sporadic throughout my life. I have found that the more mature I get though, the stronger the connection becomes. And as I have reached the stage of maturity, I feel that my knowledge and wisdom have increased. Life has taught me many lessons and some of those lessons I know come from my ancestors. For me, the important thing is to understand the lessons we are here to learn and not repeat the same mistakes over and over again. I admit that I am not perfect and have made my share of mistakes, but I also strive to learn and move in a forward direction.

I went to hear Deepak Chopra speak about his book *Super Genes*. He was talking about how we carry the DNA of our ancestors and how some of the patterns through which we live our life were actually created before we were even born. Most people

Cherokee Wisdom

don't make this connection and think everything is learned through the environment we grow up in. But I believe it is a combination of both.

For example, coming from blended cultures, when I was growing up it was sometimes confusing for me in that people often wanted to put me in a box and choose one culture or another. Since I lived in a predominantly Latino community that became the dominate culture for me even though I did not always fit in since I did not speak Spanish.

When I was exposed to my native culture though, I felt deeply connected, especially when listening to the Native American drummers. I could feel the beat to my core or maybe my soul. It was a powerful bond, one that transcended time. The drumming gave me a sense of comfort, a sense that I was not alone—a sense of feeling one with Mother Earth and the Creator.

When I think back on my life, I must have known the Cherokee connection was always there. When I was a young girl, I spent hours creating beadwork on a loom which was made for me by my Uncle Bill. I loved the art of making different designs and spent hours at a time enjoying this special hobby.

Cherokee Wisdom

I made headbands and bracelets, which I would proudly wear. It was a way of being creative and at the same time celebrating a talent from my native roots.

In elementary school I took many trips to the Southwest Indian Museum in Mount Washington, a section of Northeast Los Angeles. I always came away in awe of the weaving abilities of some tribes. The baskets were made with such precision. Some were even as small as a thimble.

I had a fascination with everything tribal–the art, clothing, customs and history. During each visit to the museum I would wonder what it was like to have lived during that time. Although the exhibits were not of my specific tribe, I still felt a deeply-rooted captivation with the life style. I often thought about my own grandmother and how the world had changed since her lifetime. In 1896 when she was born, there were no telephones, no cars, no airplanes, no electricity or any of the luxuries we now take for granted.

She was a strong woman who never spoke of the past or her life growing up. She was hard working and she and my grandfather lived on a small farm

Cherokee Wisdom

in Porterville—a small town in the San Joaquin Valley of California. My grandmother tended to the animals and kept the house in order.

As kids, my brothers and I would run around the farm. We'd go into the pigpen and play with George the pig. On one visit my grandmother made us ham sandwiches for lunch and when we were finished, she proclaimed, "That is the last of George!" I began to cry. I was devastated because as a young city girl I had not earlier made the association until that very moment that my friend George, which I had chased around the pigpen, and the ham sandwich, were one and the same. She responded, "I know you think he was your friend but he was raised for food just like all of the other animals on the farm." I was not happy about it but my grandmother still had a way of comforting me. Eventually, I came to find peace with what she had taught me.

My mother worked with the Native American community in Los Angeles for many years. She was the Native American liaison between the Los Angeles County Health Department and the

Cherokee Wisdom

Native American community. She also served as a commissioner on the Los Angeles City/ County Native American Indian Commission (NAIC) for many years. This commission was started in 1976 by Los Angeles Mayor Tom Bradley and County Supervisor Kenneth Hahn. I attended many meetings and events with my mom and had a front row seat to the activities in the community.

While in college, I worked for an educational organization called Tribal American. It provided many programs to Native American youth. I was happy to connect with so many native youth but also witnessed many of the problems faced by urban Native Americans.

Over the years I have attended many powwows, a gathering of native people coming together in celebration. I felt great joy watching the dancers glide across the arena. Fancy Dancers were always my favorite. I found them to be magical, yet mysterious. It was as if I was watching a powerful bird in flight or an animal in its natural surroundings. The dancers were a reflection of the environment and brought me even closer to my mystical roots.

Cherokee Wisdom

The drumming at the powwows was soothing as well; it felt like the heartbeat of the earth. The chanting was commanding—its rhythm powerful—and it lifted my spirits. I could not understand the words but knew they represented the voices of my ancestors speaking to me. I was mesmerized by what felt like the presence of spirits.

As an adult I was actually honored at the Southern California Indian Center powwow for being the highest- ranking Native American working for the City of Los Angeles. It was a memorable experience for many reasons. First, it was mid-summer during a heat spell with temperatures over 100 degrees. As customary for women. I wore a shawl into the arena and was bestowed a Pendleton blanket as the honoree. Pendleton blankets are used as ceremonial gifts and are made from wool—they are meant to keep you warm.

So, as I proudly danced around the arena with my mom at my side, I was sweating so much from the heat, the shawl and the Pendleton blanket that I was soaking wet by the time the ceremony was over. At the end though, despite the heat, my heart was filled with love and gratitude. I felt a pride

Cherokee Wisdom

that I had never felt before and had the feeling my ancestors were looking down blessing me. It was truly magical; I could especially feel the spirit of my grandmother which had already transitioned to the non-physical world.

Over the years I have been inspired by powerful women leaders in the tribe including Chief Wilma Mankiller who served as Principle Chief from 1985 to 1995 and Deputy Principle Chief from 1983 to 1985. She was the very first and only woman to serve in the capacity of Chief. On January 15, 1995, she received the Presidential Medal of Freedom from President Bill Clinton. *The Cherokee Word for Water* was a movie written about her life and was released in 2013, three years after her passing.

Chief Mankiller uplifted me and I was intrigued by the fact a woman could be in such a powerful position. I am sure it was not easy for her but the fact she had the courage to keep going was a true inspiration for many. It is never easy to be a trailblazer, but once a path is cleared it opens the way for others to follow.

I looked at some of the women in my own family who were courageous in their own right.

Cherokee Wisdom

Ones who lived life with passion and zest. Both my grandmother and my Aunt Sue were like this. They were people I aspired to be like. My grandmother was a quiet but strong woman having raised seven children. My Aunt Sue always lived life to the fullest and never stopped having fun. She was one of the first females to hold a leadership position in the Elks Lodge near her home. I had the honor of holding her hand as she made her transition to be with the Creator – that was a moment I will never forget.

As I have reached my 60th birthday, I feel the connection to my ancestors strengthening ever further. I recently participated in my first sweat lodge where I had visions of my ancestors dancing to the music of the scared drum. I felt so much humility to realize that I am only one small part of an expansive, eternal universe tethered to Mother Earth and bathed in the ways of the Creator. I work towards keeping this connection in life on a daily basis through prayer, meditation and my actions. I have also had the opportunity to participate in a healing ceremony where the spirits came in and helped heal a friend from cancer. There is no doubt

Cherokee Wisdom

in my mind that there is another realm where the spirits exist—I know because I have seen them.

One of my ancestors' traditions I choose to carry on is "ceremony." For me, I hold ceremonies around the Full Moon. I have a strong connection with the full moon energy. As I discussed, the moon, and all of life, operates in cycles. Since the moon is close to Earth it has powerful energy. I use this energy to release any obstacles which are hindering my personal growth, and to manifest what I want to bring into my life such as abundance, love, happiness, inner-peace, compassion or anything else I seek.

I also believe we are all energy and good energy is important. I use sage to clear negative energy through a process referred to as smudging. First, I burn the sage to clear the negativity. Then follow that by burning sweet- grass to bless the space. I have done this in my home, work space and back yard. I love the way the sage smells and I feel good after performing the smudging ritual.

I share my knowledge and the lessons from my people with the purpose that you will use it to become a great leader in your life and have a

Cherokee Wisdom

positive impact on those around you. As you travel your journey, strive to be a beneficial presence on this planet and a leader who sets a good example to others.

Cherokee Wisdom

Humankind has not woven the web of life.
We are but one thread within it.
Whatever we do to the web, we do to ourselves.
All things are bound together.
All things connect.

– Chief Seattle, 1854

TWELVE ATTRIBUTES OF LEADERSHIP ACCORDING TO CHEROKEE WISDOM

Leader **1**
Integrity **19**
Strong **32**
Humble **47**
Confident **58**
Respectful/Acknowledgment **72**
Cooperative **82**
Communicative **94**
Determined/Persistent **106**
Responsible **118**
Patient **129**
Teach **137**

One: Leader

hadatinuga

Leaders "Lead by example." Show the way by acting the way we want others to treat us.

Leadership is a topic which has been talked about over and over. There have been more than 4,500 books writ- ten on the subject from different perspectives. There are CD's, podcasts, articles and classes about the topic. My observation of life is that since human behavior is not an exact science, you cannot have a single leadership style that works for everyone. This is partly due to the fact that each person has different experiences in their life that affects how they uniquely react to the world around them.

The leadership attributes presented here are applicable in all situations. These are the same leadership qualities that help the Cherokee people fulfill their designed purpose.

Cherokee Wisdom

When we think of leaders most of us will look to famous people, ones who have had a profound impact on the world such as Nelson Mandela, Mother Theresa and Martin Luther King Jr. All are known for their greatness. Many of us think of political figures as significant leaders, as they have influenced society. They and others who bring a positive influence on many people should be celebrated for their efforts.

However, even though most of us do not consider ourselves as leaders, it is important to realize that we are all capable of doing great things. We just have to develop our leadership skills and find a leadership style that is in our comfort zone.

Most of us do not consider ourselves as leaders. The truth is we each innately possess leadership ability. In our own lives there are many times we will be called upon to be a leader. It can be anything from leading family or social circles to leading at work or in religious groups. We all have the ability to lead and at some point, in our life we will be placed in a leadership role. It is up to us to rise to the challenge and have the confidence to fulfill that role.

Cherokee Wisdom

While some people are born leaders, for others it takes time to develop leadership skills.

Leadership is also a way to take personal responsibility for our own actions. You need to understand that your actions can influence others even without knowing them or even communicating with them. I realized this through my own experience. I'll tell you a story. I was in line at a fast food restaurant one day. In front of me in line was a man—his appearance was unkempt and he was using change to pay for his food. After placing his order, he came up fifty cents short. He looked very disappointed. Without even thinking about it I handed him a couple of dollars so he could pay for his food.

What I did not realize was a mother and daughter were behind me in line. The girl looked to be about seven or eight years old. After seeing what I had done, the young girl asked her mom for a dollar. The mom gave it to her and she went up to the man and said, "Here you go. I hope this helps." We all looked at each other and smiled.

I was happy because I helped someone, but more importantly because I influenced a young girl with

Cherokee Wisdom

my actions. So, like it or not, people watch what others do and model their behavior accordingly, thus making us all leaders in our own way.

Another great example of how we can each be a leader in our daily life is the story of Rosa's Fresh Pizza in Philly. The owner, Mason Wartman was working on Wall Street when he decided to leave that career and open a pizza shop where he would sell a slice of pizza for one dollar. He named the business after his mother, Rosa.

One day a customer came in asking if anyone ever came up short of money, and if so, could he pre-purchase a slice for the next person who did? He referenced a similar approach in Italy where people can pre-purchase a cup of coffee for those who could not afford one. So, Mason agreed to it. This customer also left a note with words of encouragement for the person who would receive the free slice of pizza.

That one act of kindness grew and others bought slices for someone in need. The restaurant became filled with encouraging notes as more followed each other's example. In ten months, they gave away 9,000 slices of pizza to homeless people and to those who could not afford to buy one. Since then Rosa's Fresh Pizza has gotten national attention as more customers continue to help. These acts of kindness have gotten national attention and it keeps growing. Just another example of how we can all be leaders in our daily life.

However, not all leadership is virtuous and sometimes people use their power for destructive purposes. They convince others to follow them for their own gratification and ego rather than for the good of mankind.

A prime example of a person using their leadership for negative motives was Adolf Hitler. He was able to get many people to follow him in his inhumanity. Failing to take power by force in 1923, he eventually seized it through democratic means. He then went on to lead some of the most unspeakable crimes in modern history. This is a very extreme example, but unfortunately, we have seen history repeat itself in various ways.

As I wrote earlier, there is not a one-size-fits-all when it comes to being a leader. Everyone has his or her own idea of what leadership is. Besides, part of being a successful leader is finding a style that fits your personality. Keep in mind that your approach can vary as you adjust to a group or particular situation.

The traditional styles of leadership fall into several general categories, but are not limited to:

1. Autocratic leadership style
2. Democratic leadership style
3. Hands-off leadership style
4. Servant Leadership Hybrid leadership style —using a combination of the above

Autocratic leadership is where the person in charge is very much in command. It's "their way or the highway." An example would be in an organization where the leadership roles are very defined, such as in the military. There is no question who is the boss and that person has no problem asserting their dominance within the organization.

Democratic leadership is where the individual members' opinions are taken into consideration and the organization as a whole plays a role in the decision-making for all involved. The culture is inclusive.

Cherokee Wisdom

Hands-off leadership is where the leader lets the process unfold organically and everyone fends for themselves. If a void is created, someone steps up and tries to take charge. This style can be frustrating as responsibilities are not clearly defined. Thus, if you choose a "hands-off" style of leadership, be aware that the group dynamics can become unpredictable and uncomfortable. Here's an example of what I mean:

A few years ago, I had the opportunity to take a class at Harvard University called "Leadership for the Twenty-First Century." The class was associated with the Kennedy School of Government and was an intense one-week course with 150 high level professionals from around the world.

The first night of class everyone was excited to be there. We started with everyone going around the room introducing him/herself and the organization they worked for. The group was diverse and included a congressional representative from Africa, mayors from U.S. cities, corporate executives, non-governmental organizations (NGO's) and members of the federal government among others.

Cherokee Wisdom

After the introductions were completed the professor wrote on the chalkboard, "What is next?" He then sat down in front of the class and did not say a word. After about ten minutes of being silent, we all started to get anxious. Some even raised their hands to speak but he did not respond to them either.

As his silence continued, the class grew more uncomfortable. Thirty minutes into his silence a few took it upon themselves to take charge and start a discussion. They decided to call on those who were raising their hands. They assumed since it was a leadership class they should jump in and show leadership. But their assumption did not bear a lot of fruit.

In fact, a few of the participants became angry and asked the professor to "do something." One person said, "We paid good money for this class. You need to teach us." But he still did not respond. Another person decided he was going to take on the role of professor—that is until he realized he did not know how to do it.

This went on for an hour and at the end of the class the professor got up and walked out.

The students found themselves feeling unhappy, anxious and angry about the situation. The next morning the class discussed what had happened and the conclusion most people drew from the experience was that if there is a void in leadership chaos can occur.

My take-away from the experience was, if you choose a "hands-off" style of leadership be aware that the group dynamics are unpredictable and not everyone will be comfortable.

Personally, I tend to change up my style based on who I am working with. This places me in the hybrid leader category. But I always maintain my core values as guideposts.

VALUE DRIVEN LEADERSHIP

Over the years of developing my own hybrid style, I have come up with a general description of how I operate. I call it **Value Driven Leadership**. What I mean by this term is as long as I make decisions from my core values, I will never make a bad decision for me and I will be able to sleep at night.

Cherokee Wisdom

I acknowledge that not all of my decisions have turned out the way I had hoped they would. But that doesn't mean they were bad decisions. Just ones based on the information and awareness that I had at that time. I also acknowledge that not everyone will like my decisions. But then again being a leader is not about a popularity contest. When you are working with a number of people there is a high chance of making at least someone unhappy. This is especially true when you need to make difficult decisions that affect many.

A friend once told me when you are a leader, statistically 10 percent of the people affected will not be happy with your decision. That reality was intimidating when I had oversight over 5,000 employees and realized that 500 people would not be happy with my decision, no matter what I did.

But that is something I need to accept as a leader. And so, do you. That is why making my decisions from my core values allows me to be comfortable with the choices I make. Knowing that tough decisions are sometimes for the greater good helped me live with the fact others might not be happy. I have found too that many times when people are not happy with my decision it is not always about the decision. It is often about them being unhappy over something that is going on in their life and projecting their feelings onto me. As a leader I have had to learn to not take their unhappiness personally.

I am convinced that the Value Driven Leadership style works equally for everyone because most of us have the same core values. The delivery may come across as dis- similar because we each have unique personalities, but the process is the same.

FEARLESS

I believe as a leader you need to be fearless. Do not be afraid to take risks. If you allow fear to get in your way you can hinder the progress of the group.

The people you are leading usually feed off of your energy. So, if they sense fear or uncertainty from you, they will not want to move forward. However, if you are confident and secure in your decisions, they are more apt to follow your lead.

Cherokee Wisdom

Fear is a powerful emotion and can impact people's behavior. If you only stay within your comfort zone you will likely miss out on opportunities for greatness – for yourself and for others. There are many types of fear which can prevent progress:

- Fear of taking risks
- Fear of the unknown
- Fear of failure
- Fear of success
- Fear of conflict
- Fear of public speaking
- Fear of social rejection

The list goes on and on. Fear also comes in different degrees starting with an uneasy feeling all the way to immobilizing terror. We all experience some level of fear—just don't let it stop you from being a leader or succeeding.

Cherokee Wisdom

NIMBLE

Being nimble means making adjustments and changes as needed. You can have the best plan in place but there are always going to be unforeseen circumstances that arise. A good leader is able to make the proper adjustments and keep going. We can plan and plan but life happens and things can change in a split-second that make those plans obsolete. Having the ability to change course can be the difference between becoming stagnate or becoming successful.

WOMEN IN LEADERSHIP

For years women have typically been in leadership roles when it comes to family and community. As a matter of fact, the Cherokee tribe was based on a matrilineal society.

Fortunately, though, over the last few decades many women have also stepped into leadership roles in their careers, becoming top corporate executives and elected officials among other positions with greater responsibility. There is a debate as to whether or not their leadership style is different. I don't have a definite answer on that one, but I do believe if women are afforded opportunities, they can be excellent leaders by applying which ever style best suits them.

I do know that as a female leader you are looked at differently. If a male is a dominating leader he is called "powerful." If a woman is a dominating leader she is called "emotional." I think as more women take leadership roles; our society will become more accepting of them. Thus, it will make it easier for more women to step into top leadership roles.

In the field of politics, I have observed that women tend to be less ego driven and more results oriented. This does not mean that women elected to public office don't have egos. But my observation is that women politicians tend to be less involved with scandals such as bribery and sexual indiscretions. One may argue that that is purely a numbers game. There are fewer women politicians so fewer of them can be involved with the political drama. Time will tell if my perceptions are accurate.

As a woman who has held many leadership roles I realize that I have been put under the microscope

Cherokee Wisdom

more than my male counterparts. For example, when I was President of the Board of Public Works for the City of Los Angeles managing a department of over 5,000 employees, many times I was the only woman in a meeting. As the person in charge, and being a woman, I understood I had to work twice as hard. I had to make sure I was prepared for every encounter and had to have a solid foundation for my decisions since I would be under extra scrutiny.

In meetings I had a habit of going around the table and getting input from all the staff present before I made a final decision. I would ask everyone for his or her input regardless of their job title. Then I would make what I thought was an appropriate decision. I could see on some people's face they were not happy with my decision. I did get a lot of "Well, we have never done that before" so I would smile and say "Let's just try it my way and we will revisit it if it doesn't work."

I am convinced that the Value Driven Leadership style works equally for both genders because most of us have the same core values. The delivery may come across as dissimilar because we all have unique personalities but the process is the same.

Cherokee Wisdom

LEADERSHIP LESSON #1

Leadership principles are simple when you remember to treat others how you want to be treated, lead by example and use your core values as a guidepost.

Wisdom from Abraham Bearpaw (Bear)

>>> **Leader** <<<

Some leaders are borne out of necessity while others create their own space to lead. Whatever your motivation or circumstances; a capable leader must first take care to make sure their own house is in order. We must find out what motivates us to lead and take into account our strengths and limitations.

If we find ourselves wanting in a particular area then we take the necessary steps to remedy those deficiencies. Whether it is our lack of training or lack of education, we must put in the work to make sure we are prepared for our leadership role. Then having taken inventory, we are ready to proceed fully knowledgeable of and confident in our

Cherokee Wisdom

abilities. "Fake it until you make it" is a popular mantra of new leaders but it is unnecessary if you are willing to put in the work to build up your skill level.

Preparation is often a reliable indicator of success for leaders as talent alone will only get you so far. I found this out the hard way in my life also. I was willing to dream but unwilling to make the necessary sacrifices at times to make my dreams a reality. So, in the game of life I am very mindful that hard work often trumps talent.

Cherokee Wisdom

*If you want to achieve success
in whatever you set out to do,
You have to start as though you are
hand-in-hand with all of creation.*

Keetowah Saying

Cherokee Wisdom

Two: Integrity

kaliwohi

Integrity, as defined by the Cherokees, is doing the right thing even when no one else is around.

Taking action which is in alignment with our core values is a way of life. After all, we each know the difference be- tween what is right and what is wrong. Most of us will make good choices when other people are watching. Knowing someone else is witnessing our behavior somehow holds us accountable. But the true test of integrity is doing the right thing when no one else is looking. That can be challenging for some people. You are the only person you have to answer to when no one else is around. No one else will know if you do something that is inappropriate.

Cherokee Wisdom

We usually refer to this as our conscience. We have all seen the visual of someone trying to make a decision and on one shoulder you have an angel telling them to do the right thing whereas on the other shoulder there is a little devil with a pitchfork telling them to do the wrong thing. This visual portrayed in the media in the struggle people may go through when making a decision.

Others equate integrity with honesty; if you are honest you have integrity. And some consider having integrity to be a matter of respect for yourself as well as for others. Essentially, you respect yourself enough to do the right thing.

I believe it is a combination of self-accountability, honesty and respect. Plus, the Creator always knows your heart–so when you accept that and believe in a power bigger than yourself it is easier to act with integrity.

Let's look at a hypothetical situation as an example:

You find a wallet on the ground. You look around and there is no one else around. You pick it up and open it. Inside you find a driver's license, credit cards and $500 in cash.

Cherokee Wisdom

What do you do?

You have several options:

1 You can do nothing – put it back on the ground and move on.

2 You can take the cash and then return the wallet to the owner with the driver's license and credit cards.

3 You can take the cash and credit cards and use both of them, and then return the wallet to the owner with the driver's license.

4 You can keep the cash, credit cards and driver's license and not return the wallet.

5 You can contact the owner or authorities and return the wallet with everything intact.

Factors to consider:

>>> If you use the credit cards or driver's license that will be illegal – someone will possibly find out in which case there will likely be consequences to pay.

>>> If you take just the cash that will be dishonest – but you will almost certainly get away with it.

If you return everything intact you will be acting with integrity.

In this hypothetical situation I would ask myself, if I lost my wallet what would I want someone else to do? Of course, the answer is to return the wallet with everything in it. So that is what I would do.

But there are some who will say "Take the cash" and "If no one else knows why should I care?" Or, "It is only a crime if you get caught." Or, in trying to justify what they do by saying, "Well I found the wallet so 'finders' keepers, losers' weepers.'"

Ultimately, the decision will be yours to make and you will have to live with the consequences. Even if you return the wallet but keep the cash, you may think you have done "mostly" the right thing, but you may have to live with the guilt. If you do not feel guilty though there are still karmic consequences. So why keep something that is not yours? Besides, you don't know the circumstances of the person who lost the wallet. Maybe they need the money to buy groceries, pay rent or medical bills. They could be a single parent struggling to survive. You just never know.

Cherokee Wisdom

The fact of the matter is you should be authentic and true to yourself no matter what the situation. Being authentic means not lying to yourself or to others. No one else may know but you will know and those experiences, good or bad, will stay with you. If you make good choices you can be more fortunate.

At some point you will be put in a situation that tests your integrity. It is likely you will be tested many times throughout your life. It is your choice on how you deal with this and it is your responsibility to accept the consequences.

Keep in mind no one is perfect and there may be times in our lives when we might make different choices. But the important thing is we learn to make choices from a place of integrity. Strive for the good choices to outweigh the bad ones. By acting with integrity, you will feel good about yourself and that will help you develop other skills such as confidence, trust and inner peace.

You might ask yourself do people really give back the lost wallet with the money in it. Well, the answer is yes.

Cherokee Wisdom

Here's a true story that highlights these values: A 7-year-old boy in Salem, Massachusetts was with his uncle playing at the park. The boy found a checkbook with an envelope in it, and in that envelope was $8,000 in cash. He showed it to his uncle and his uncle wanted him to learn an important lesson: "Treat people the way you want to be treated."

So, they went to the Salem Police Department where officers were soon able to track down the owner of the money. This owner gave the little boy one hundred dollars as a reward. One hundred dollars is a lot of money to a seven-year-old, yet the lesson his uncle taught him about integrity was priceless. Yes, there are people in this world who do operate with integrity.

There are going to be times in your life as a leader when your integrity may be challenged. Doing the right thing as a leader is not always easy and sometimes it can be a painful process. However, maintaining your integrity is always the right thing to do.

Several years ago, when I was serving as a policy maker on the Board of Public Works for the City of

Cherokee Wisdom

Los Angeles, we had a controversial project come before the commission for project approval. At the time, the voters of the city had passed a bond measure to build new fire stations. The challenge was where to build these new stations since Los Angeles was very populated and there was not a lot of open space. Some of the areas where there was the most need had the least amount of space to build.

One particular project was needed to service the resi- dents in the Hollywood Hills. The community opposed the location for the new station. Many of the people opposing the project were my friends. One in particular met with me and asked me to stop the project.

As the project went through the approval process, hundreds of people attended a particular commission meeting in opposition to the project and things got ugly. Emotions ran high and not very nice things were said to me. As I was listening to the people opposing the project though, I was mindful to respect their opinions. Once all of the information was in, I chose to maintain my integrity and realized the new fire station was a public safety issue and could not be compromised. I did understand that some businesses and residents might be impacted during the construction of the project, but I had to look at what was in the best interest of the city as a whole.

So why do so many people have trouble with integrity? We live in a society that promotes individualism and not community. We think about ourselves first and other people second, if at all. Some are taught to get ahead at any cost including fooling ourselves into thinking that immoral behavior is okay and getting over on the system is a good thing.

I am not here to judge anyone and I also understand that no one is perfect. I certainly have had moments in my life when I did not make the best choice. But the important thing is that I have grown as a person and striven to make the best decisions I am capable of in every situation. Learning lessons is a part of life. The key is to learn from the experience and not repeat the same mistake over and over.

One area where many people struggle with the issue of integrity is in business. If you are all about making a profit and at the same time you are hurting others, you are actually hurting yourself too.

I am certainly not saying that profit is a bad thing. It's just that I have seen companies cut corners to make a profit while not worrying about the consequences. For example, there was a company selling faulty air bags on automobiles. Finally, after several years of this, there was a recall of millions of the airbags. This situation resulted in the largest auto recall in history. The defect was eventually revealed but only after several injuries had occurred. An investigation showed that the company and the car companies they supplied to may have already known about the problem for up to five years.

It is my belief we live in an abundant society and there is plenty of money to go around. I also believe you can have an organization which has values and makes a profit; the two are not mutually exclusive. So, there is both personal integrity and corporate integrity.

But at the end of the day everything starts with personal integrity. If you have that, then all areas of your life will be transformed—family, friends, and work.

Cherokee Wisdom

LEADERSHIP LESSON #2

As a leader, strive to keep your integrity and do the right thing in all situations.

Wisdom from Abraham Bearpaw (Bear)

>>> Integrity <<<

Most people define integrity as "doing the right thing even when nobody is around." This is important as leaders must have legitimacy to be effective. While it is true that employees will follow instructions just so they do not get in trouble, those that believe in their leadership are more productive. It is unreasonable to expect perfection from anyone but if those in your charge have questions about your integrity then your ability to lead is diminished. Where you once found unquestioned loyalty, you might now be met with skepticism at every turn. This affects the entire chain of command and slows down production considerably as gossip and backbiting among team members can now take root. The best thing is to act with integrity at all times so that others have faith in your decision making.

So, what happens if you do something out of character and there are now questions about your integrity? Well, all is not lost provided that you are willing to take the necessary steps to fix the situation. First and foremost, you have to be prepared to take responsibility for your actions and be accountable. In our society most people are willing to forgive; though it does depend on the transgression. Next it is important to communicate to others what corrections are being made as transparency will help to rebuild trust. People respect honesty and if you are willing to own up to your mistake, correct it and keep the lines of communication open then there is reason to be hopeful that you will move past any integrity issues.

In the past there have been instances where I made mistakes and had to apologize and make corrections. While many see apologizing as a sign of weakness, I feel like I am a much more effective leader because of it. Those that I supervise feel comfortable that I am always acting with their best interest and the best interest of the organization

Cherokee Wisdom

at heart. I have also heard that they respect me more knowing that I made mistakes but acted with integrity to own up to those mistakes and correct them. We all make mistakes but it is how we handle them and learn from them that really matters.

Cherokee Wisdom

Be strong when you are weak.
Be brave when you are scared.
Be humble when you are victorious.

—Native American Wisdom

Three: Strong

utlanigida

**Be strong in whatever you do.
Take comfort in the strength of the
Creator and of your ancestors.**

As leaders we are the backbone of our organizations and need to be strong. However, we must develop our own strength before we can be strong for others. This strength has several elements: mental, physical, emotional and spiritual.

MENTAL STRENGTH

The mind is a powerful tool. I believe if you set your mind to something you can accomplish it. Having this mental strength revolves around believing that what you want to accomplish is doable–that believing you can reach your goal even when it seems impossible. This is easier said than done because our brain has been programed with many negative thoughts as to why we cannot reach our goals. For instance, life experiences create guilt, shame, anger, resentment, and insecurities–all which can interfere with our mental resolve. Our life experiences, good and bad, can also have an impact on our mental abilities.

One of the tools which I use to gain mental strength is the practice of positive affirmations. Positive affirmations are a way of reprograming the brain to eliminate the negative thoughts which hold us back and replace them with constructive beliefs.

Speaking from my experience, I was the first person in my family to go to college, which was not easy because my family did not have the finical resources to even buy me a book. I was traveling through uncharted territory without much support. No one in my immediate family knew how to help me and so in my senior year of high school I went to visit a college advisor. He did not give me any encouragement at all. Actually, just the opposite. He told me, "College is not for you. Go get married and have children like the rest of your friends."

I had to find the mental strength to have faith in myself and figure out mostly on my own a way to go to college. The college applications themselves can be cumbersome and complicated.

By tapping into my mental strength, I was able to continue to believe in myself. I worked several jobs, took out student loans and struggled to keep going. I saw many of the students around me drop out for a variety of reasons. And after years of being determined, I at last received my master's degree from the local state university when I was twenty-three. When I graduated, I did not feel like I was better than anyone else, but did feel proud that I had kept going despite the many challenges and obstacles.

PHYSICAL STRENGTH

Physical strength involves taking care of your body by eating healthy and exercising. I cannot say I have always adhered to this lifestyle. But the more mature I get; I have gained greater appreciation for the importance of this and have realized that without good health the quality of my life will decline.

Cherokee Wisdom

In many communities of color there are significant health challenges such as heart disease, high blood pressure and diabetes. Most of these heath issues are caused by an unhealthy diet and lack of exercise. Although there is not really a cure for diabetes, it can be controlled by taking the proper steps.

In addition, according to the American Heart Association, in the United States about one in three American kids and teens are overweight or obese. This obviously has an impact on their physical strength, but also can be controlled by taking proper steps.

In 2014, when I was fifty-eight years old, I set a goal for myself where I needed to tap into both my physical and mental strength. I was asked by a friend to join her for her fiftieth birthday celebration by participating in the Avon Walk for Breast Cancer. The Avon Walk financially supports finding a cure for breast cancer. It was a two-day event in Santa Barbara, California. I agreed to do the first day, which was 26.2 miles (a marathon) and make a commitment to raise money ($1,800) through sponsors.

Cherokee Wisdom

Twenty-six miles may not sound like it would be that challenging to walk in one day. Well, let me back up by saying when I was very young, I was diagnosed with "Club Feet" and from the age of about four to six years old I wore orthopedic shoes to correct the problem. Throughout my childhood and into my teenage years I was plagued with severe pain in both legs, which the doctor called "growing pains." Fortunately, by the time I was an adult the problem corrected had itself and I rarely experienced the discomfort that I did as a child. However, the thought of walking 26.2 miles brought back some of those old memories—but it was for a good cause and I had made a commitment so I pushed through. Nine months prior to the event I began training in preparation for the big day. I was part of a group of four women and we all agreed to support each other in taking on this challenge.

On the day of the event I felt physically prepared, but what I was not prepared for was that for twenty of the twenty-six miles I would be walking alone. For a variety of reasons, the other women either had dropped out or I did not see them on the route. It was an extremely hot September day and it took me a lot longer to do the course than I had anticipated. During the last five miles my body was getting tired. Not only did I need to tap into my physical strength, I also had to search deep for my mental strength.

During the last two miles the heat from the burning asphalt started to become overwhelming. But just when I started to think about giving up, I saw a young girl holding up a sign which read, "When your legs get tired, walk with your heart." That message came at the perfect time and gave me the lift I needed to keep going and successfully cross the finish line to enjoy the sweet taste of victory. Never mind that it took me eight hours. Not only did I help raise money for a great cause, I was able to complete the goal despite my history as a child.

EMOTIONAL STRENGTH

To be emotionally strong is to have the ability to face whatever is put in front of you with dignity and perseverance. On top of that, it is important to recognize that we are spiritual beings having a human experience. As a result of the human

Cherokee Wisdom

experience, everyone faces various challenges in their life, some more than others.

In my experience, emotional strength is sustained by building a support network. This support system then helps us keep going while we manage the challenges put in our path.

It has been my observation that women are better at creating a support system for themselves than are men. Women tend to find support with family, neighbors, co- workers or friends. Men on the other hand tend to congregate with other men around a specific topic such as sports, hobbies or careers. In addition, some men have difficulty sharing their emotions as they perceive that as a sign of weakness.

It is important for everyone to have a safety net since each of us have circumstances in which we are faced with challenges, obstacles or hardships. The challenges can come in many forms, including a significant change or loss of someone or something.

Having emotional strength will not change the circumstance but it will help us cope with it. For example, when we experience a loss there are several stages of grief including denial, anger, bargaining and depression before we get to acceptance. Loss is not only having someone make his or her transition, it can also be an end of a marriage or a loss of a job.

In my life I have had times when I needed to turn to my support network for help in dealing with losing loved ones, going through a divorce or being displaced from a job. Because life is dynamic, you never know when you will find yourself in a situation where you need to be strong emotionally. Having people around you providing you with unconditional love can help you uncover your emotional strength.

SPIRITUAL STRENGTH

Let me start off by saying that I do not believe there is one way to look at the topic of spiritual strength. I feel your views are individual to you and I encourage you to find what works best for yourself; there is no right or wrong way to believe. For me what works best is being in alignment with the universal consciousness. This makes me a better person and a better leader.

Cherokee Wisdom

I believe in God, Creator, Universal Consciousness and Infinite Love. It does not matter which name you use. I believe it is a power greater than myself, and one which I connect to on a daily basis. I also recognize there is a difference between spirituality and religion. I am certainly not suggesting one is better than the other and acknowledge each person must find his or her truth.

For me, I consider myself to be spiritual and not so much religious. I feel that I have a direct connection with the Creator. I can tap into that power through prayer and meditation at any time. I describe the difference between prayer and meditation as follows; Prayer is talking to God and meditation is listening to God. For me I need both to be in balance and harmony and at my optimum.

You too can gather strength knowing that you are connected to something bigger than yourself—as well as by accessing through prayer and meditation the power, knowledge and wisdom of your ancestors.

One of the best discussions on spiritual strength I have heard was at a panel discussion I attended on the topic of Business and Spirituality. The panelists were a very diverse group:

Cherokee Wisdom

Speaker 1

Sri Sri Ravi Shankar is a spiritual leader and founder of the Art of Living Foundation which has a message of love and compassion. The Art of Living Foundation is in 156 countries, is considered the world's largest volunteer-based Non-Government Organization (NGO) and has assets in the millions.

Speaker 2

Rob Dyrdek is an American professional skate boarder, entrepreneur and an MTV star. He is passionate about building skateparks so young people can have a safe place to skate and stay off the streets.

Speaker 3

John Paul DeJoria is an American billionaire businessman and philanthropist best known as the co- founder of the Paul Mitchell line of hair products and Patron Tequila. He is known for helping the environment and many humanitarian causes.

At first, I found the mix of these three leaders to be very unusual. At face value they are so different. What they have in common though is they all have a belief that you can be successful and be committed

Cherokee Wisdom

to making the world a better place, each in our own unique way. The presentation was very inspiring and well received by the standing room only crowd. My take-away from the experience was not only are we all leaders, but we each can be successful and spiritual at the same time. I personally consider all three of these individuals to be cutting edge leaders tapping into their spiritual strength.

The opposite of strength is weakness; we have all felt vulnerable at some point in our life. When we feel weak, we can turn to the Creator knowing that whatever obstacle or challenge we are experiencing is only temporary and that the circumstances will pass. Just like in the dark of the night you are guaranteed that there will once again be light.

Your strength is not only for yourself to draw on but also for the others in your life too when they are feeling weak. Sooner or later everyone will experience a loss of a family member, friend, neighbor, co-worker or all of the above. By turning to the Creator, you will understand that although this person's physical body is no longer here, their soul/spirit continues to exist in the non-physical world. Being strong for others in their time of need is an important part of being a leader.

Cherokee Wisdom

LEADERSHIP LESSON #3

The best leaders are the ones that develop a combination of mental, physical, emotional and spiritual strength.

Wisdom from Abraham Bearpaw (Bear)

>>> **Strong** <<<

Native people have long been able to persevere and prosper due to our self-care and our commitment to each other because therein lies our strength. In the previous section we talked about integrity and the role it plays in our ability to effectively lead others. However, integrity is also an integral part of the foundation that makes up our self-respect, which, along with our physical, emotional and spiritual wellness will determine how strong we are. Self-respect is important because when we believe that we deserve good things then we will make decisions that help us get to a positive outcome.

Since time immemorial our self-care was built into our society and daily living. Gratitude is a central value we share and we start the day with

Cherokee Wisdom

a prayer of thanks. Also, throughout the day little affirmations serve to maintain a healthy outlook. Cherokees believe that it is important to think positive thoughts while we braid our hair, cook our food and make baskets or do other crafts. This is because our positive energy is transferred to whatever we our doing. This is similar to the saying "made with love". However, this positive thinking also aids those performing the task because they program the mind to be positive and allows us to focus on what is important.

Our strength is derived from equal parts what we do plus what we consume. Getting enough rest, exercising regularly and eating healthy puts our body in optimal shape to perform at a high level. Consuming positive material, keeping an attitude of gratitude and practicing mindfulness enables us to be more effective decision makers. Our ability to stay well and balanced determines our strength level on a given day and we must make the decision to be well daily. When I am well and balanced then I make good decisions, I care for everyone and I have abundant energy. When I stray from my wellness routine then I feel anxious, tired and judgmental.

Cherokee Wisdom

One tell-tale sign that I need to improve my wellness is when I feel like arguing with people on the internet. I know this is a warning sign because when I am well and strong then I want to lift people up instead of argue with them.

Keeping a journal is a great way to keep an eye on your warning signs and will help you stay on the path to wellness and remain strong.

Cherokee Wisdom

"We can no longer afford to support separation among peoples, separation within self, or separation from our past and future, honor."

Crosslin Fields Smith
Cherokee Elder & Healer

Cherokee Wisdom

Four: Humble
eladi yadadvnedi

Be Humble. Never boast; never think you are better than anyone else.

Humility means not thinking you are better than anyone else and realizing we are all human just doing the best we can. We each have our own journey in life and lessons to learn. Just because the next person's journey is different does not make them better or less than you, just different. Many of the attributes I am discussing are common to most cultures but humility is often overlooked.

We each start as a baby dependent on others for our nourishment and care. Thus, the ideas about being better than others are learned later in life.

In the United States we live in an ego driven

Cherokee Wisdom

society which teaches us to be competitive and push to be number one. This can lead us down a path of forgetting how to be humble. It is okay to be competitive and strive for greatness—but just be competitive with yourself, not with others. Remember too that trying to do your best and be your best does not require you to compare yourself to other people.

Some people fall into the trap of thinking just because they have wealth, they are better than others. That a bigger house, an extravagant car, expensive shoes or designer clothes makes them superior. I remember seeing a bumper sticker saying "The person with the most toys wins". I am still not sure what they win. Money may provide access to more opportunities but it does not make you a better person. Nor does money buy you happiness. Having money does not even allow you to escape the cycles of life. We all leave this planet in the same way making a transition out of our physical body. Having money will not spare you from making that transition. Don't get me wrong. There is nothing wrong with abundance, as long it does not give you the illusion that you are better than anyone else.

Even with this insight, we still find many who they think they are better than everyone else. This often happens with those in careers where we as a society idolize them, such as actors, athletes, politicians, or musicians.

But once they make a mistake and it becomes very public, we then realize they have many of the same problems we all do. They may also have a whole different set of problems we are not aware of. For instance, you hear on the news about famous people getting stalked by their fans or the paparazzi. It is not their entire fault that such importance is placed on them, forcing them to live in a fishbowl. However, with all of the attention, some of it self-created, it may be a challenge for them to stay humble because of the way everyone treats or reacts to them.

Holding an impressive job title in front of your name also does not make you better than anyone else either. A job title is what you do to make a living, but it still does not save you from the natural laws of the universe. In fact, you may be the boss at work but your success is due in large part to the people around you. People quite simply are not successful alone.

Cherokee Wisdom

Actually, we each may have different ideas of what success looks like. Some people may feel successful if they are doing what they enjoy for a living; others may feel successful if the people they love surround them. Both are right, as are many other genuine views on what success means. Yes, we each get to define success in our life, however, just keep in mind achievement does not make you better than the next person–just different.

Another word associated with humility is modesty. Modesty comes from the word moderate. When you do things in moderation your life is in balance. So, when you are out of balance with the emotion of humility, you are filled with ego. You can also think of it this way–the opposite of humility is arrogance. When your ego takes over you can become self-obsessed and self-important. This can drive people to take competitiveness to the extreme and want to win at all costs, including putting other people down or even going to the extreme of hurting them physically. In these cases, competing gives the illusion they are better than the other person if they "beat" them.

Cherokee Wisdom

Other people fall into the trap of thinking they are better because they are of a particular race or culture or ideology. For example, look at what is going on in the world with terrorism—a small group of people have a belief that their ideas are better than everyone else's and they are willing to kill hundreds of people to prove that point. How can their beliefs be more valuable than people's lives? The entire notion just boggles the mind. The concept of religious wars is so extremely flawed because if you believe in God (or any higher power), how do you justify killing other people?

In contrast to this, the idea that we are equal is the foundation for humility. And it is a lesson we need to reinforce all the time. In the Mexican culture there is a beautiful story of the Virgin of Guadalupe (Virgen de Guadalupe), the patron saint of Mexico.

The message of her story is simple, indigenous people are equally loved by God and therefore should be treated as equals to contemporaries. Her story first started at a time in history during which the indigenous people were viewed as less than because of the color of their skin and their unique philosophies that were different from their conquerors.

Cherokee Wisdom

According to tradition, the Virgin Mary appeared to an indigenous man named Juan Diego on December 9, 1531. Official Catholic accounts state that the Virgin Mary appeared four times before him and one more time before his uncle. She asked Juan Diego that a church to be built at that site where she appeared to him. So, he took the message to the church, and only after a miracle happened, the priests finally believed him and the church was eventually built.

The Virgin of Guadalupe is beautifully depicted with brown skin, an angel and moon at her feet and rays of sunlight that encircle her. Today, The Basilica of Our Lady of Guadalupe is the most visited Catholic pilgrim- age site in the world, and the world's third most-visited sacred site. What her story represents is a sign of equality and humility.

Sometimes life has a way of humbling you. One of the most humbling experiences I have had was when I was in college. I was working on my Master's Degree and was only twenty-two years old at the time. I was committed to being a good student and strived to get a 4.0 grade point average in the program. My youthful ego may have been getting inflated since I was doing so well in school. I participated in a study group with three other students; two of the students were Asian and the other one African American. We studied together for the mid-term exam, which was a take home test. After the mid-term, I got called into the professor's office and he said I had not passed the test. I was mortified and asked why, since I thought I had done well and knew I had studied very hard. He replied, "It is obvious you cheated off someone else's paper since you and Henry (the Asian male) have the exact same answers." I had not cheated and did not realize until then that it was the other way around.

The humility came when I realized that I was being judged on being a young Latina/Native American woman, and not on my abilities. I promised the professor I had not cheated and asked him to hold any judgment until the end of the course and I would prove to him I was capable of good work. He reluctantly agreed and by the end of the course he did admit that he had made a false assumption about me—though he never apologized. I did have him for two other classes and did well.

Being humble and living in balance with the world assists you in understanding that we each have an equal place on this planet.

LEADERSHIP LESSON #4

A leader can be humble and confident at the same time.

Wisdom from Abraham Bearpaw (Bear)

>>> Humble <<<

Humility is an important Cherokee value that helps us to remember that we are only a part of the universe and not the center of it. While society today steers us toward selfishness and narcissism; humility helps us to stay grounded and connected to others. There is no doubt that being humble has advantages for the ordinary citizen but how about those who are in leadership roles?

Many people may think that leaders needn't worry about being humble but humility actually helps leaders to be more effective in several ways.

Cherokee Wisdom

Leaders who are humble often remain teachable, are able to learn from their mistakes and value input from their team. There is nothing worse than a leader who cannot take suggestions from others or admit when they make a mistake. This behavior sets a poor example for the team and may lead to division among team members.

So how can we put being humble into practice? First, we can take comfort in the realization that we aren't perfect and will definitely make mistakes from time to time. Knowing this takes some of the pressure off and helps us relax in our position. Next, admitting when you make a mistake demonstrates transparency and lets the team know that you value honesty over perfection. This allows team members to operate with ease and makes them more productive. Also, pointing out team member's strengths and contributions instead of your own will make them feel valued.

I have struggled with humility in the past because I would often put on a front of over-confidence to mask my shortcomings. However, this set me back as I was just masking my self-doubt and other inadequacies instead of working on them. Soon this

Cherokee Wisdom

over-confidence gave way to full blown narcissism and I was on my way to accomplishing nothing while feeling as though the world revolved around me. I wasn't accomplishing anything because my exaggerated sense of self made me think that I didn't have to work as hard as others because I was "talented". I also missed out on a lot of great ideas because I thought that I already knew everything. It was my Cherokee culture that saved me from that toxic cycle when I began to follow a wellness program. First, I had to accept that I wasn't so talented and smart that I could get away without hard work. Next, I began to value and praise others for their contributions which helped foster relationships and made me feel more connected. Finally, I was able to accept that I only know a little which is awesome because it means I get to keep learning for the rest of my life. All of these things have made me more accepting and effective as a leader because I can relate to others and help them instead of putting myself above them. Being humble helps me daily but like everything else you have to make the decision to work at it every day.

Cherokee Wisdom

*Looking behind, I am filled with gratitude,
looking forward, I am filled with vision,
looking upwards I am filled with strength,
looking within, I discover peace*

—Quero Apache Prayer

Five: Confident

udadohiyuhi

Have confidence in yourself. Do not doubt your abilities, but temper all with humility.

CONFIDENCE

Confidence is complex yet also simple. A belief in your- self that you are capable of what you want to accomplish and capable to follow your dreams is essential to finding meaning in life. Our confidence usually is connected to our self-esteem. So, if our self-esteem is healthy, our confidence levels are usually good. If we are having issues with our self-esteem though, it is difficult to feel good about much of anything.

Confidence and self-esteem in adulthood are usually influenced by our experiences when we were growing up. If someone tells us we cannot do something at a young age, it can have an impact on how we see ourselves and what we tell ourselves later in life.

The opposite is also true. If we are told as a child, we can do anything and be anything then we tend to develop a higher level of self-confidence. Parents, grandparents, extended family or teachers play a vital role in influencing our inner beliefs.

SELF-ESTEEM

Self-esteem reflects a person's overall subjective emotional evaluation of his or her own worth. It is a judgment of oneself as well as an attitude toward the self. Self-esteem encompasses far-reaching belief systems, for example, "I am competent" or "I am worthy."

The opposite of being self-confident is possessing little self-regard. This can lead those who suffer from this state of being to become depressed, to fall short of their potential, or to tolerate abusive situations and relationships. It can also cause them to them to question their abilities and be filled with fear or uncertainty.

A sense of well-being runs on a spectrum across various degrees. For instance, on one end of the spectrum is confidence and self-love; on the opposite end is arrogance with an off-putting sense of entitlement and an inability to learn from failures.

The extreme form of arrogance is narcissism. The defining feature of narcissism is the desire to maintain a grandiose sense of self. Narcissists think they are very special people indeed and want everyone to know it. Most people want others to like them, but narcissists want others to admire them for their greatness. Many narcissists even have good social skills, appear self-confident and charming and are very assertive in promoting their own interests. They also tend to be highly competitive, and try to derogate those they see as rivals. Typically, they respond very aggressively to insults and perceived slights. Narcissism is selfishness and is negative, that is why we must temper all with humility.

On the surface it can appear that confidence

and humility are in conflict. So how do you build confidence yet stay humble? The answer is in finding a balance along the spectrum where the opposite emotions are in harmony with each other. This involves reprogramming our brain with different beliefs. We need to tell ourselves we can accomplish our goals and follow our dreams but at the same time have the awareness that doing so does not make us better than anyone else. Those are your dreams and you worked hard to achieve them. However, they are just that, yours. The next person may have different dreams and they are to be equally respected.

Another influencing factor on us, and in particular on our youth, is the media. Society sets standards through the media standards which shape the way we view ourselves. If you are a young girl and all you see are beautiful models that are a size zero, you start comparing yourself to them, which can leave you feeling bad about yourself. You may start to feel so bad that you go to extremes to look like them. Research shows this kind of societal pressure has played a role in eating disorders being on the rise amongst girls and young women. The reality is in the

United States the average dress size is between 12 - 14. So why do we push the idea that everyone should be a size zero? The pictures you see in magazines have taken a lot of work to get them perfect. First, there is a team which works with the professional model—the team includes a hairstylist, a make-up artist, a photographer and a wardrobe stylist. Then once the picture is taken, it is altered by using such tools as Photoshop through which the model's appearance is adjusted to give a slimmer waist, whiter teeth or even greater height. The point is a lot goes into that one image. So, to compare yourself to what you see in the magazines is having unrealistic expectations. It leaves us with a feeling of not being good enough. I believe as long as you are eating healthy and exercising you should be whatever size is healthiest for you and your body type.

The same goes for men with pressure to have a muscle-packed physique. Boys in particular have a tendency to compare themselves to professional athletes. It has been exposed that some of the top athletes have used steroids and other performance enhancing drugs, which gives them an advantage. This is not to say all athletes use drugs— most achieve their greatness through hard work. It is good to have heroes and positive role models but not ones that don't play by the rules or have integrity.

If you fall into the trap of comparing yourself to others, it is a no-win game. Each and every one of us is unique and special just the way we are. Albert Einstein did not speak until he was four years old and did not read until he was seven. His parents thought he was "sub-normal," and one of his teachers described him as "mentally slow, unsociable, and adrift forever in foolish dreams." He was expelled from school and was refused admittance to the Zurich Polytechnic School. He did eventually learn to speak and read but he developed at his own pace. Today he is known as a genius.

Another factor which can influence your confidence is worrying too much—worrying about what other people think or worrying about things that might happen. The first is particularly true for students in middle and high school. At that age, everyone is doing his or her best to fit in and no one wants to be perceived as an outsider.

Recently I was facilitating a workshop for some girls and had the opportunity to spend quality time with them. Some of them were in middle school and much of their conversation centered on what the other girls at school thought about them. So, I asked one of the girls why she was so worried about the other girls' opinions. She looked at me with bewilderment and said she was not sure. I told her not to worry about what others think, just be true to who she is. She smiled and agreed.

If you are a worrywart it is almost impossible to be confident because you are too busy thinking about all of the harmful things that might happen. Besides, researchers have found 85% of what we worry about never even happens. In addition, worry places your focus on the future rather than on the current moment. Live in the present and enjoy today.

Finding this balance between confidence and humility can be delicate. You don't want to be arrogant yet you also don't want to be perceived as weak.

One way to help with this balance is to surround yourself with people who will be honest with you and who will tell you the truth through constructive criticism. I have seen individuals achieve a position

Cherokee Wisdom

of power and then surround themselves with a group of "yes" people who agree with all their ideas, good or bad. It may be nice for their egos but it can keep these individuals removed from reality. It reminds me of the Hans Christian Anderson story of "The Emperor's New Clothes." When the emperor paraded around in his new clothes, no one dared to say that they didn't see any suit of clothes until a child cried out, "But he isn't wearing anything at all!" No one wanted to tell the emperor the truth except a child. You don't want to be the emperor.

So, develop a good support system around you. It can be friends, family, coworkers, neighbors or anyone in your life who will be honest with you. I understand that not everyone has a good relationship with or lives close to his or her biological family members. However, we have a choice to pick the people we want close in our lives to provide support.

Several years ago, I met an amazing woman named Shirley Roberts. She was very involved in Los Angeles politics and lived her life with zest and passion. She was never married and did not have any children, but she had an amazing group of people in her life she called her family. I was fortunate enough that she included me in her family and even called me her niece, though we were not blood-related. I learned so much from her and when she made her transition, I had the honor of holding her hand until she got to the other side.

The biggest lesson I learned from her was that we have choices in life and regardless of the circumstances, you can choose your "heart family." They may not be your biological family, but you can love and enjoy them just the same. We do not get to choose our biological family, but we can choose the people we have in our life to share good times, sorrows, and life experiences, as well as to help keep us grounded with humility. When Shirley thought someone was getting out of balance and filled with too much ego she would say, "They needed a belly button check." What she meant by that is we all have belly buttons and no one is better than the next, so don't let your ego get too big no matter what you're doing. She had the opportunity to know some very influential and wealthy people and she would tell everyone the same thing.

Cherokee Wisdom

Sometimes in life it can be difficult to have confidence in yourself, especially at a young age. However, if you don't have confidence in yourself, who will? There have been many times in my life when I had to put myself out there and just go for it; to walk through my fears and step outside my comfort zone. For example, when I was in college, I ran for student council. I decided to run for a seat which represented the women on campus. At first the thought of campaigning and asking people to vote for me was intimidating. I had to find the confidence within to know that I was not only capable of running but also of winning. I made posters and fliers and stood in the center of campus asking strangers to vote for me. I was only eighteen at the time, but I knew that I had the ability to do a good job. I won the election and it was a great experience which built my confidence. It also gave me the opportunity to speak in public. And I found the more times I spoke in front of crowds, the easier it became.

Cherokee Wisdom

LEADERSHIP LESSON #5

A great leader strives for humility through keeping the ego in check yet remains confident when working toward the task at hand.

Wisdom from Abraham Bearpaw (Bear)

>>> **Confident** <<<

In the last section we expanded on the topic of humility but how does that square with being confident? Can we be both confident and humble? Yes, we can and our humility can actually help us to be more confident and more decisive. It is important for leaders to be confident as nobody wants to follow someone that doesn't believe in themselves. A confident leader reassures their team members that they are in good hands which makes them feel more comfortable and able to trust their decision making. Let's take a look at the process of becoming more confident and how it can help in our leadership roles.

Cherokee Wisdom

First, we need to look at ways to grow our confidence and then we will learn how to use it effectively. Growing up I did not have a very high level of self-confidence and I was content to be a follower rather than a leader. I was the classic scholarship kid; always willing to share what I thought others wanted and expected to hear from me. However, my confidence began to grow the day that I was finally able to accept myself and be authentic. When I stopped doing what others wanted and began to pursue my own passions then I really started to feel my confidence rise. I did face challenges in my quest for confidence, however, as I was not accustomed to sharing my true self and had to develop new skills.

For instance, a skill that I needed to turn my dreams into reality meant that I had to become a proficient public speaker. The very thought of this however, would make my palms sweat and heart race. When I was in high school, I won a writing competition and almost fainted when I had to read out loud what I had written. So, how was I to become better at this when it terrified me so? Practice is how I did it. I had to practice a lot to

Cherokee Wisdom

become better and I took every opportunity to get up in front of others and speak. I started by just speaking in class and at staff meetings which was scary but made me feel good also. Over time I began to feel more comfortable speaking to larger and larger groups and even though I was nervous every time I was also very proud of myself even when it didn't go according to plan. Now, I am regularly asked to speak at conferences and other engagements which is awesome because it allows me to share my experience, strength and hope with others.

Cherokee Wisdom

"We will never have true civilization until we have learned to recognize the rights of others."

—Will Rogers

Cherokee Wisdom

Six: Respectful/ Acknowledgement

tsudadanilvtsati

Respectful/Acknowledgement hold one another scared.

RESPECT

Respect and acknowledgement are interconnected.

Respect is a word that gets used often, but what does it really mean? If you look at the formal definition: "it is a feeling of admiring someone or something that is good, valuable or important. A feeling or understanding that someone or something is important, serious and should be treated in an appropriate way."

Cherokee Wisdom

It means I am able to accept that you to have your own thoughts, beliefs and ideas while also not imposing what I think or believe onto you. I accept you to live your life without judging or discriminating against you. I understand that what you believe matters. I understand that you have the right to your opinion. I might not agree with it, but that is what you believe based on your life experiences.

We all have different life experiences that shape us. We are all individuals and have our own uniqueness. For instance, you can see two people grow up in the same household but they still come out with different ideas, thoughts and beliefs. That's because even though people can share in the same situation, when they look through their lens of their life, they will see it from their individual viewpoint. That doesn't make one better than the other. It just makes them distinctly individual.

A perfect example of this is when there is an automobile accident with several witnesses. Each witness gives their account of what they saw. Each version may sound very different since everyone is giving his or her specific account of what happened.

Cherokee Wisdom

In addition, each person may have viewed the accident from a different angle and is only able to give their perception of what they saw. Add into the mix that the drivers may also have a different version since they are giving their individual perception of what happened. Even though there may be different accounts, each person may still be telling the truth based on his or her individual understanding of what the truth is.

Respect then is about embracing differences and accepting each person to have their respective opinion without proving that you are right and they are wrong. In applying this to leadership, when a leader is respectful and respected, he or she has a better chance of being effective. On the other hand, if the leader is not respectful and respected it can be challenging to have the others follow their direction or instructions.

People often feel disrespected when their beliefs or ideas are not honored. So, remember, everyone is entitled to their opinion.

You can respect a person without having to agree with them. One example that comes to my mind is about a woman who has been a trailblazer in Los Angeles politics, Gloria Molina. During her political career she accomplished many positive things for the community, and I have a lot of respect for her. She was the first Latina to be elected to the California State Assembly in 1982. She went on to be the first Latina to be elected to the Los Angeles City Council in 1987. In 1991, she continued to open doors by being the first Latina elected to the Los Angeles County Board of Supervisors where she served until the end of 2014. However, many people have questioned her leadership because she has an autocratic style. Despite this, she was able to accomplish many great things and open the door for others to have opportunities which were not there before. I have much respect for her and acknowledge her efforts on behalf of the community.

ACKNOWLEDGEMENT

We all want to be acknowledged. If we feel acknowledged that gives us a sense of value.

Acknowledgement and validation are one in the same. Validation is having other people express that you matter.

Cherokee Wisdom

That what you think is important. When you validate someone's ideas or opinions you reinforce their power.

Throughout our life this can be extremely important. In school, for example, we want to be acknowledged for our efforts from teachers or other authority figures. This validation can come in the form of grades, awards or praise.

Later in life we seek validation from our bosses, co-workers or customers. There was a period in my life when I worked for the government. The employees who worked in the department I was assigned to could not be rewarded with additional money or raises even if they did a good job. This was because of specific civil service rules which needed to be followed. What I did find though is that many times when an employee went above and beyond the call of duty, they appreciated acknowledgement, praise and a simple "Thank you." The acknowledgment was a validation of their efforts and their hard work. Feeling appreciated was a strong enough reward and they continued to excel.

Validation is a key factor in developing self-worth and building confidence. What happens sometimes is if you do not believe exactly the way someone else does, your own opinion can seem to you to have less value. The truth is we all have the right to our own opinion. Once you understand that we are each unique and have own value we can start to hold one another scared.

Even though we all have the right to our own opinions, it can cause issues when one person wants to impose their beliefs onto other people. Or when the ego gets involved and one person wants to be right or prove the other person wrong.

When taken to the extreme it can result in war. I feel war is saying: "I do not respect you; I want to impose my ideas onto you or to take your resources and will do this at any cost. I want to change you into believing what I think is right."

When I was a young girl, the Vietnam War was erupting. I remember watching the nightly news and they would list the names of the soldiers who had been killed that day. I was deeply affected by this since I realized each name on the screen was a person's life. I would also see many people protesting the war, which caused more confusion. I asked those around me, "Why are all those people dying? What is the war about?" I became really sad because I could not get a straight answer from any of the authority figures in my life.

Today when I look back, and I think most people would agree, there wasn't a good reason for all those people dying. It was a senseless war which left thousands dead and many lives damaged. The war lasted almost 20 years and cost the U.S. billions of dollars. To me this was the ultimate disrespect to our veterans, their families, Americans, and the people of Vietnam. After the war ended, we then tried to repair some of the damage. But that did not change the fact we had not respected those most affected or held them sacred.

HOLD ONE ANOTHER SCARED

What does it mean to hold one another scared? One of my spiritual sisters, Jeannie Estrada (aka Sister Weeping Willow) explained it this way: "That which you cannot buy is scared." She went on to say, "Love and happiness are sacred." So, when you hold someone in a scared place it is a special reservoir with respect, love and compassion. This is not to be confused with placing them on a pedestal and not having them be held accountable for their actions. Obviously, if they disrespect you or treat you in a negative way you should distance yourself from them.

To be clear, I am referring to holding people sacred. Not material things. Do not mistakenly worship money or non-living entities.

LEADERSHIP LESSON #6

As a leader, be respectful to the people you are working with and acknowledge them for their ideas. Hold them sacred so they may flourish.

Wisdom from Abraham Bearpaw

>>> **Respect/Acknowledgment** <<<

Respect is an integral part of not just Cherokee culture but Native Culture as well. This common value has enabled Indigenous people to inhabit this continent since time immemorial without becoming over burdensome to the environment. It was out of respect that we only took what we needed and left the earth as we found it. We acknowledge that all of creation has a place in this world and we respect that symbiotic relationship so that we may walk in balance.

These values hold true for any organization and it is important for leaders to show respect and acknowledge the contributions that others make. Respect is contagious in an organization and others will begin to act accordingly which will lead to a positive working environment. However, leaders should also put this virtue into practice at home in order to create a nurturing home environment that is conducive to cooperation. When others feel like their contributions are acknowledged and respected then they are more willing to be creative and dream big.

Cherokee Wisdom

The best way I can describe the teaching of my people is "A complete comprehensive respect for life and creation that has no end."

Crosslin Fields Smith
Cherokee Elder & Healer

Cherokee Wisdom

Seven: Cooperative
dilisdelvdi

Help one another

COOPERATION

Few people accomplish anything independent of others. We are social creatures by nature and as a result we interact with others all the time. To be an effective leader you must learn the skills of cooperating with others or you may have trouble reaching your goals. We need cooperation in relationships, work, government and in just about every aspect of our lives.

Working with others is not always easy though, partly because we each have our own ideas and thoughts. So, it is not about coming up with ideas

Cherokee Wisdom

and making others do what you want. But rather it is more effective if you co-create the plan with other people so they can buy into it from the beginning. Since people tend to be more cooperative in a reciprocal relationship with give and take on both sides, with this emotional investment they are also more likely to excel at achieving the goals that have been set.

An important lesson many need to learn when working with others is you do not need to be right all of the time. Also, people don't like to be bossed around. Some can even get stubborn if they feel bossed around and want to prove they are right no matter what the circumstances are. This usually causes them to stop listening because they have already made up their mind. The person on the other side of the conversation may have a good point to make but the one who is offended can become so set on proving they are right; they close themselves off to other opinions.

It is particularly important to be open in romantic relationships and long-term friendships. Being right can mean nothing if you drive the other person away. This goes hand in hand with learning

Cherokee Wisdom

to say you are sorry when you are wrong. One thing I know for sure is that no one is perfect and no one is right one hundred percent of the time. So, taking the high road and learning to apologize when you are wrong or at fault is a big achievement.

And just like everyone makes mistakes, also no one knows everything despite what some people think about themselves. That's one reason why it is important to know you can usually learn the most from a conversation when you are not talking and are open to listening to the other person's views. When listening to others and letting them be heard you strengthen the relationship too.

We have all heard the saying "It takes a village to raise a child." Well in order for that child to thrive, the village needs to cooperate. If the caregivers are not cooperating with each other, the child may become confused by mixed messages. Cooperation over parenting becomes even more important in today's world where so many marriages end in divorce. In those situations, the adults have to learn to cooperate and adjust to a new lifestyle for the sake of the children.

Cherokee Wisdom

In addition, the parents divorcing need to be very aware of their children's feelings and cooperate as much as possible to limit the impact of the change (divorce) on the kids. Speaking from experience, it is not always easy but you can learn to cooperate with your ex even though you may not like them.

Unfortunately, I have seen many examples of parents who are in the process of divorcing who do not cooperate and in fact irresponsibly put their children in the middle. It is not fair to make the children choose a side, and it is indeed very harmful to try to manipulate them. They are not at fault and should not be made to feel so, either directly or indirectly.

When I was seven years old my parents divorced. It was a very ugly split and my mother was quite vocal in saying negative things about my father. For the most part my father took the high road, but he had other issues including not being dependable. As in most of these situations, I am sure now both of them played a role in the cause of their divorce, but as a child I didn't care about who to blame. I just wanted the pain the whole family was feeling to stop.

Cherokee Wisdom

Though neither of my parents was perfect, the negativity voiced by my mom had unnecessarily long-term effects on everyone involved.

So as an adult when I found myself going through a divorce, I tried my best to cooperate with my son's father and not say negative things. I am certainly not saying I was perfect, but I will say I made an effort knowing what impact the negativity could have on my child. He grew up to be an incredible man and I am very proud of him.

At times, cooperating with those in the work place, with family, or elsewhere can be challenging. The key is for all to recognize that it takes both sides, not just one person, to work toward common ground.

With that said, you may find yourself in a situation where others do not want to cooperate with you. Usually it is because of their issues, not yours. The important thing is that early on you realize this and decide how you want to handle the conflict. You don't have control over other people's actions, only your own actions. What you do have control over however is how you participate with them. So, if you find yourself in a situation where the other person is not able to cooperate, take the high road and walk away.

HELP ONE ANOTHER

In today's world there are so many people all over the globe in need. There are the homeless, people dying from starvation and HIV and a lack of clean water. There are refugees fleeing their war-torn homelands, and the list goes on. It can be overwhelming just trying to figure out who to help. It does not matter how big or small though, just help someone. Do what feels right to you, but do something.

I have personally learned the importance of helping others and I do this with both my time and resources. I understand that this can be a big step for many people because we get caught up with our own lives and our own issues. But when you help others it comes back to you in so many unexpected ways. I call it the law of reciprocity. I have found that the more I give, the more I get. This is not to say I give with an expectation of getting something in return. But rather when I have given from

Cherokee Wisdom

my heart, I have received blessings beyond my imagination. When you too give from a place of compassion without expectations, you will find the universal law returns the blessing.

I believe that most of us do want to help others and the trend seems to be headed in that direction with people of influence and wealth leading the way. Microsoft founder Bill Gates and his wife Melinda Gates with their creation of the "Bill & Melinda Gates Foundation» has been identified as the world's wealthiest charitable foundation with assets reportedly valued at more than $34.6 billion.

Billionaire Facebook founder Mark Zuckerberg and his wife Dr. Priscilla Chan celebrated the birth of their baby girl with the stunning announcement they plan to give away most of their fortune through an initiative to "advance human potential and promote equality for all children in the next generation." They pledged to give away 99 percent of their Facebook shares in their lifetime, currently worth about $45 billion.

Warren Buffett, who was worth over $62.6 billion at the end of 2015, has pledged to give away 99 percent of his wealth. These people with so many resources have made a conscious decision to help others.

There is now an official day of giving called "Giving Tuesday" which refers to the Tuesday after Thanksgiving in the United States. It is a movement to stimulate generosity and in 2015 it brought in almost $40 million to organizations that serve a variety of causes.

But you do not have to be a billionaire to help others. There are many ways to help. If you do not have money, you can help others with your time. Giving your time can help others in so many ways to improve their lives.

The other advantage of giving is that it feels good. When I am helping others, I get a sense of satisfaction and enjoyment. For example, for the past several years I have been involved with a program called Girls Today Women Tomorrow (GTWT). It is a non-profit leadership mentorship program based in Boyle Heights, California. It services young Latina girls from the ages of 10 to 22. GTWT provides support, positive experiences and mentors to these young women so they can set goals and follow their dreams. Many of these young women live in under-privileged communities filled

Cherokee Wisdom

with poverty, violence and abuse without a clear path to success so the opportunity is often life-changing. By participating in the GTWT programs, most of the young women go on to attend college and enter into careers they otherwise might not have been exposed to, such as engineering or business. In fact, most of the girls are the first person in their family to go to college. As I see these young girls blossom into leaders, it gives me a sense that I am making a difference in their lives and I feel good.

The GTWT program also encourages these young women to cooperate with each other to provide a support network. It can be a difficult time for a girl attending middle school or high school. Indeed, without the support of the program it can be unbearable for many of them to maneuver through the pitfalls of being a teenager in the inner city. Add to this mix that teens can be cruel to each other. Cyber bullying, for instance, has taken this cruelty to a whole new level since there is limited account- ability. With the GTWT program they establish close friendships with other girls. And they learn valuable life lessons which they carry with them in building a quality life for themselves and their loved ones.

So, by cooperating with others you will find that your life will be enriched as well as will be the lives of the people you help. Through cooperation we can make both our society and the planet a better place.

LEADERSHIP LESSON #7

A true leader will cooperate with others and find the wherewithal to help people.

Wisdom from Abraham Bearpaw

>>> Cooperation <<<

For much of my life I was only concerned about my own point of view and I would often rather be right than be effective. I am fortunate that I was able to relearn how to be cooperative and come to realize that we can do anything if we work together. Indigenous people have long known the value of being cooperative with each other in order to survive fierce adversity. Being cooperative has now allowed these Tribes to not just survive but thrive.

Cherokee Wisdom

Being cooperative lends value to modern day leaders as well. Those who are willing to reach across the spectrum and work for a common goal are often more successful than those who operate on an island. Like everything else, however, being cooperative is a choice that we make every day for the betterment of our organizations and families. Ego is an ever-present obstacle to overcome in the pursuit of cooperation but it is possible if we choose to be effective instead of being right.

Cherokee Wisdom

"The Cherokee Way is to be of service to others, to be mindful and care for all living beings. We have our own version of the Golden Rule; we are to treat others how they want to be treated without regard for how we are treated. This allows for true growth of others and ourselves. Before we were called Cherokee, we were AniGaduwagi, the people that rise above, and we certainly have and this way of life is to be an example for others. We rise as communities and through working together."

Dawnena Squirrel
**Cultural Outreach Officer
Cherokee Nation**

Cherokee Wisdom

Eight: Communicative
Didadvgododi

Be Communicative and be sure to let others know

COMMUNICATION

Few, if any, of us are mind readers so we need to communicate with other people to express ourselves and articulate what we are thinking and feeling. On the other side of that is receiving the information, which we do by listening and that then enables us to understand what other people are trying to communicate.

Sounds simple enough, right? Well, communication is not always as easy as it sounds. Words have different meanings and can signify different things to different people. In English the same word can have multiple meanings. For example, the word write sounds the same as right but with different spelling and significances.

Since we all have different experiences and as a result see things from our own unique perspective, this reality can influence our perception of a specific word.

To complicate it further, in society there are phrases or slang that get incorporated into our communication. This jargon changes and evolves on a continuous basis. For example, someone talking about an actor and his role in a movie might use the phrase, "He killed it" meaning he did an excellent job. Another person might feel there is a negative connotation to that phrase since to kill is not a good thing. And since there might also be regional differences in the way people express themselves, some words used on the West Coast may have different meanings than the same words used in the North. For instance, in California "mob" is slang for get over here quick by foot, bike, car, skateboard. Just get here. In New York though "mob" clearly means organized crime, or a crowd of people.

Cherokee Wisdom

There are also cultural differences depending on where the person was raised. Some people assume that Spanish is a consistent language. Well, it is not because there are so many countries which speak the language. If you speak Spanish with someone from Spain it is very different than if you are speaking Spanish with someone from Cuba, Mexico or Argentina. Each country has its own dialect and jargon.

The United States is a melting pot of over 200 languages which are spoken in addition to English. We have all heard the saying "lost in translation." There is some truth to that, including English to English, since the person doing the interpreting is using their experience and knowledge to process what they are hearing.

An example of the uniqueness of some of the native languages is during World War I the U.S. military used the Cherokees and other tribes to communicate secret messages. These brave men where known as code talkers. They would transmit tactical messages back and forth and the enemy had no understanding of what they were saying. In September of 1918, the first recorded code talkers

Cherokee Wisdom

were from the Cherokee nation. The Choctaw were then utilized and the program expanded to many other tribes. The code talker practice carried over to World War II where the Navajo were primarily utilized.

Another factor which has had an impact on the way we communicate today is technology. Technology is a double-edged sword. It has connected the world at some level yet at the same time it has limited in-person interaction. Technology is a good thing but we would be fooling ourselves if we thought it did not also adversely affect our language, culture and communication.

Social media platforms condense communication even further. For example, on some platforms there are almost no written words communicated – instead everything is done with pictures or videos. Your thoughts and feelings are transmitted with hashtags and emojis. I have no judgment when I point this out because I utilize most social media platforms. It is just an observation that deeper communication is very limited.

The way we communicate through texting can be even more challenging since those messages tend to be in an entirely new abbreviated language. For example, LOL means "Laugh out loud." This appears to be a language that not everyone understands and is evolving all of the time. "143" means 'I love you." "182" means "I hate you." DBAU means "Doing business as usual." There is clearly a generational difference at play as generally the younger you are the more attuned you are to this medium.

In addition to verbal and written communications, there are non-verbal communications. Emotions can be communicated through nonverbal communication such as crying or laughing. When someone is crying, we know they can be either sad or happy depending on the situation. How you are feeling can also be expressed through body language or even just through a look.

I have been known to communicate nonverbally with my eyes. I remember when I was raising my son, all I had to do was give him a certain "look" and that could shape his behavior. He knew that a certain look was of approval or sometimes disapproval. Anyway, he certainly got the message loud and clear without me saying a word.

Cherokee Wisdom

Infants also communicate nonverbally long before they even learn to talk. For instance, parents can tell when their baby is hungry or needs to have their diaper changed.

If you have pets, you become familiar with their non- verbal communication too. My dog knows how to get my attention without making a sound. I know when he wants to go outside, when he wants to be fed and when he wants to be petted.

Now back to humans. Even though we are of the same species, men and women communicate in different ways. Studies have shown that men use fewer words in a day vs. women. It has been claimed that women speak about 20,000 words a day — 13,000 more than the average man. That certainly does not make one better than the other, just different.

Generally speaking, men are about analyzing a situation and getting right to the solution. While women might find it soothing to talk it out and discuss their feelings associated with the issue.

Women have a tendency to talk about their feelings to better help understand them and deal with them.

Cherokee Wisdom

Of course, you will find exceptions to every rule but the point is to be aware when you are communicating with someone of a different culture or gender–there are differences.

In today's society men can find it difficult to talk about their feelings and emotions, though this seems to be improving. We all remember the book from the 1990's "Men are from Mars and Women are from Venus" by Dr. John Gray. That book was a cultural phenomenon selling more than 50 million copies and was the "highest ranked work of non-fiction" of the 1990s, spending 121 weeks on the bestseller list. Why was it so popular? Because it was one of the first times people accepted the idea that men and women are not only physically different but also that our brains are wired differently and we communicate differently. Neither way is right or wrong. Just different. Finding productive ways to communicate with the opposite sex is an art and takes patience. However, finding that good balance can eliminate a lot of problems. Make sure you are not only listening to what other people are saying but that you are understanding them as well.

Cherokee Wisdom

Communication also gets misinterpreted when you have many people involved. When I was a child in elementary school, we would play the telephone game. The children would sit in a circle and the teacher would whisper a statement in the first student's ear. The statement could have been something like "Tommy is going to the park after school." Each student would whisper to the next student what he or she heard. By the time it went around the circle the last student would say out loud what they heard. It always came out distorted such as "Tommy is afraid of the dark and a pool."

The students would all laugh and think it was so funny. The point is the more people involved with a message the higher chance of miscommunication since each person adds their perception. They might hear something different or put their own interpretation on it. That is also the way rumors get started–each person passing along the message they hear which can get changed. So be mindful when you hear something second- or third-hand. It might not be what was originally intended.

The tone and level of your voice can also influence communication. Some people think if they speak louder you will hear them. I know if someone is raising their voice or yelling at me it has the opposite effect. I actually tune them out.

Communication is never going to be perfect and there will always be miscommunications. There are several steps you can take though to improve communication with others. First, make sure you are clear on what the person is saying. Second, try not to assume things and instead clarify what you are unclear about–for instance, ask them, did you mean this? Are you saying this? This allows your communications to flow more easily with a clearer understanding of the conversation.

LISTENING

Listening is considerably underrated. If you do not take the time to listen, how will you ever be able to receive another person's communication?

If you are talking, you are probably not listening. We have all heard people describe a situation where someone says, "I was not able to get a word in edgewise." When another person is not willing to listen, when they make the communication one-sided, it can be very frustrating.

Cherokee Wisdom

We all have an obligation to participate in effective mutual communication, which involves both relaying thoughts and information and receiving the other person's communication. Now I am not saying that you have to agree with what the other person is saying. All I am suggesting is that for effective communication you need for both sides to be heard.

LEADERSHIP LESSON #8

As a leader it is imperative you are both effectively communicating and listening to your group.

Wisdom from Abraham Bearpaw (Bear)

>>>Communicative<<<

One of the most important virtues of a good leader is to be communicative. A good leader actively participates in dialogue with those in their charge. Sharing your vision and direction is important for others to be able to fulfill their obligations more efficiently. While this clarity of

Cherokee Wisdom

expectation is needed, equally important is for information to be relayed to leadership about the needs of team members. When there is an open line of communication between leadership and team members then this cuts down on delays and misinformation that can create obstacles to optimum performance. Leaders must also take care to not just use this line of communication for direction, however. It is also important to regularly recognize the contributions of the team and convey the importance of their input.

It is a challenge for me to communicate with others at times. As a younger man I did not feel as though what I had to say was important. Negative thoughts still creep in from time to time and try to take away from what I have accomplished. However, because I use the tools that I have learned I can communicate with others so that I do not live in my head and let negative thoughts run me. I also really enjoy sharing positive communication with others to let them know that they are valued.

Cherokee Wisdom

The secret of our success is that we never, never give up.

Wilma Mankiller
Cherokee Nation Principal
1985-1995

Cherokee Wisdom

Nine: Determined/ Persistent
nidvdayosgvna

Determined/Persistent means never giving up

DETERMINED

Determined means being tenacious or strong-willed and not giving up when obstacles arise. When you are working on a project or goal, inevitably there will be challenges because nothing in life is perfect. The key is to work around the obstacles or challenges to figure out a solution and keep moving forward.

If you are the leader and you are managing a team working toward a goal this becomes extremely important because if you give up, the rest of the team will quit as well.

Cherokee Wisdom

When I do public speaking, I always say "Anything is possible but that you need three ingredients to reach your goal:"

1 You need to believe it is possible
2 You need to take action and do the work to make it possible
3 You need to never give up

Sometimes people believe their dream is possible but they don't want to do the work required. Others do the work but they don't believe their dreams are possible. Once you believe and do the work by taking action, the final step is to be persistent. Stay determined and focused until you get there. This last step tends to be the most problematic for a lot of people.

Many give up when their pursuit does not happen in the timeframe they have set in their mind. Many want things to happen when they want them to happen and do not want to be patient for the results. After all, we live in a society with a short attention span that thrives on instant gratification. We do not like to pay our dues or wait for things; we want things to happen now. But once you realize you do not control time or when things blossom, you will begin to realize everything happens when it is meant to. The easy thing to do is give up; the more difficult thing is to keep going when you cannot see the end in sight. Having faith in what you are doing is a powerful lesson to learn.

When people do give up, they have the tendency to play the victim role. But this victimization takes away from your personal power and diverts you from your dreams and goals. One thing for sure, if you give up you will never get where you want to be. If you keep going though, you will achieve the goal if it is meant to be.

Being determined means not allowing the outside influences to sway you away from what you know is right for you. Your vision and dreams are just that, yours.

The people around you may not see your vision and therefore not be supportive, but you should not allow them to get in your way. For example, this tends to happen with parents and their children. The parents have certain expectations of what they want their children to do with their lives. They want the best for their children. Some want their them to grow up to be doctors, lawyers or have careers generally associated with making money. The children, on the other hand, may be creative talents and want to be singers, artists or actors. In truth though, a parent's role is to give their children a solid foundation (education and morals) and then support them as they make their journey through life.

If we as parents try to control our children's destiny and manipulate their lives, it can backfire and cause problems. When I was a young adult one of my co-workers was pregnant. She announced, "My son is going to be a dentist." I asked, "How do you know that?" She said, "I have his entire life planned out. He will go to this university and will have the career I have chosen for him." According to her, dentists made a lot of money and she wanted her son to be successful.

The problem with that scenario is she was determined, but for someone else, not for herself. It is amazing that in this day and age there are people who still think they can control the life of another person. Yes of course parents have the right to their opinion, but a plotting out a predetermined life does not usually go smoothly.

PERSEVERANCE

Perseverance means always working toward your goal and keeping going until the task at hand is complete. As a leader, you many have team members who quit or not pull their own weight. That is a separate issue. But as the leader everyone is watching you. Your role is pivotal and so your perseverance sets the tone for others to follow. Or even offers the inspiration for them to find their second wind.

When you hear some of the great leaders speak, they will talk about how many of their biggest challenges have also been their biggest teachers. There are lessons in every challenge, and obstacles, not matter how disruptive, can bring opportunities—admittedly, we may not understand the lesson or opportunity until much later.

Cherokee Wisdom

Think about how different our world would be if everyone gave up. There are many successful people who failed countless times but did not give up:

For example, Walt Disney formed his first animation company in Kansas City in 1921. He made a deal with a distribution company in New York in which he would ship them his cartoons and get paid six months down the road. Unfortunately, he was forced to dissolve his company and at one point could not even pay his rent. By persevering though he went on to build one of the biggest entertainment empires of all time and his legacy lives on to this day.

Thomas Edison's teachers told him he was "too stupid to learn anything." Later, he was fired from his first two jobs for being "non-productive." And then as an inventor, Edison made 1,000 unsuccessful attempts at inventing the light bulb. When a reporter asked, "How did it feel to fail 1,000 times?" Edison replied, "I didn't fail 1,000 times. The light bulb was an invention with 1,000 steps." It is all about perspective.

In Cherokee history Sequoyah was a great leader who invented the Cherokee Syllabary. He would go off into the woods and spend hours alone over a several year span of time. People began to think he was crazy because he did not tend to his crops or do what everyone else was doing. Others thought that during the time he spent alone he was in communication with the spirits.

But then in 1821, he completed the Cherokee Syllabary of 85 symbols that represented almost all of the sounds in use at that time in the Cherokee language. And as soon as the alphabet was accepted by the tribe, he was celebrated and hailed as a hero. The United States treasury department even provided him with a sum of money in recognition of his accomplishment. He went down in his- tory as one of the most famous Cherokees. My first uncle was named after him, his middle name being Sequoyah.

The list of famous people who had initial failures and then go on to do great work is very long. What they have in common is that they did not give up. They lived by the saying, "If at first you don't succeed, try, try again."

So, when you have your ideas, dreams or passions, do not let anyone or anything steer you off your chosen course. If all of these inventors and creative geniuses had given up, think how different our lives would be today.

Be persistent with your dreams and goals but also be open to learning from your challenges and obstacles. Thus, persistence and stubbornness are not the same so when you are working toward a goal do not get the two confused. A leader needs to be nimble and adapt when obstacles arise. So, don't get stubborn and set in your ways to the point that you lose your ability to adjust the plan.

In my life I have had the good fortune of being sur- rounded by effective leaders, ones I have observed and learned from. A good friend of mine, Antonio Villaraigosa, became the 41st Mayor of the City of Los Angeles. I was a big supporter and active in his campaign.

Villaraigosa was a seasoned politician and had served in the California State Assembly since 1994 and was elected as the 63rd Speaker in 1998. His opponent was also an experienced public servant; James Hahn who had served as city attorney and city controller.

Cherokee Wisdom

The race for mayor was a tough fought battle and despite the fact that Villaraigosa had built a very diverse coalition, he lost to Hahn in 2001. The Villaraigosa supporters were in disbelief and felt devastated as they watched the election returns. Villaraigosa did not give up though. He persevered and four years later he did the impossible. He was able to unseat the incumbent Mayor Hahn in 2015, and by doing so was elected as mayor of the second largest city in the United States where he served two terms. Not only did he win, he became one of the most influential Latino leaders in the country.

His persistence was inspiring and helped me learn the lesson of never giving up. The other important lesson I learned from him was how a small book can change your life. After he lost the first election in 2001, he gave me a copy of The Four Agreements by Don Miguel Ruiz. That book helped me understand the simplicity of life and the importance of ancient wisdom. Since then, I have had the same book signed by Don Miguel Ruiz and both of his sons and it remains one of my most valued possessions.

Cherokee Wisdom

When you are leading others, being persistent can be difficult for a number of reasons. But one of the main ones is just due to the dynamics of the group. When you lead people, understand that everyone is going to have their own opinion. There may be people in the group who do not believe the goal you set can be accomplished. If they voice negativity, it can spill over and create doubt and uncertainty amongst the others. So be determined to not let their negativity get you off track. Once you set your goal, firmly believe it can be reached. Then do the work and never give up and your dreams can come true.

LEADERSHIP LESSON #9

As a leader move your team toward the finish line by being determined, persistent and never giving up until the goal is accomplished.

Cherokee Wisdom

Wisdom from Abraham Bearpaw

>>>Determined<<<

For me, the topic of being determined can be summed up with a quote by my aunt, Wilma Mankiller. She said "The secret of our success is that we never, never give up." This is true of not just Cherokee people but all indigenous people who have persevered in the face of extreme hardship and adversity. As I sit and write this now the world is reeling from the coronavirus pandemic. However, all over the world there are leaders that are emerging and showing how determined the people of the world can be. Social media has turned a spotlight onto the daily struggles of determined families across the world. What I see is family after family who are determined to be positive, determined to be helpful and are determined to care about others. So, while this is definitely a scary time for the world. I take comfort in the fact that the majority of the population are determined to be of service.

Cherokee Wisdom

" I like to be able to raise people's consciousness, yes. And to remind that those of us involved in the receiving end of the oppression, we have a duty."

–Wes Studi

Ten: Responsible
adudalvdi

Commit yourself to your task or assignment

Just as you need to be persistent you need to take the work seriously and be responsible.

When I think of the word responsible, several words come to my mind: accountability, dependability and commitment. These words are very similar but each has its own meaning.

ACCOUNTABILITY

Accountability comes in two forms — being accountable for yourself and holding others accountable for their actions.

Being accountable means keeping your word, which goes hand in hand with having integrity. The

Cherokee Wisdom

people around you need to know that your word means something and that they can depend on you to follow through on assignments. You need to be viewed as being trustworthy that you are a person of your word. If on the other hand you are not responsible, people are not going to take you seriously. If you promise to do something but do not keep your word, people will start losing respect for you.

In a group situation other depend on you to do your part and if you do not follow through it may impact the entire team. I remember it could be frustrating when I was in college and a professor would give us group assignments. It was great if everyone followed through. But when you had a student who did not pull their weight it had an impact on the entire group and sometimes our grade.

Here's another example on accountability. At the end of 2015, comedian Steve Harvey hosted the Miss Universe Pageant and made an epic mistake. He inadvertently announced the wrong winner—on live TV he said that Miss Columbia was the winner. She received the flowers, was bestowed the beautiful crown and pranced around the stage waving to the cameras.

Cherokee Wisdom

Steve then came back onto the stage and corrected his announcement. He apologized and said he had made a mistake and that the real winner was Miss Philippines. I was watching the show live and must admit it was one of the most awkward moments I have ever seen.

However, that night Steve Harvey gained my utmost respect because he took responsibility for his actions and apologized. He did not blame it on someone else, he admitted his error. I am sure it was not easy for him because his mistake happened in front of millions of viewers all over the world. Social media went crazy and he was criticized by many people. It got so out of control he claimed that his family had received death threats after the incident. Still, he showed the world how to be a man with integrity and be accountable for his actions.

That is what I will remember about the incident.

The next part of this equation is holding others around you accountable for keeping their word. This is not to say you have control over other people's actions, but if someone does not keep their commitment you need to bring that to their attention. You cannot force other people to do their task or assignment, but you can question them about their lack of follow-through. At first, they may get defensive, make up excuses and not take responsibility. However, if you do not question their lack of follow-through you are indirectly participating in their behavior. Plus, you are actually helping them because they may not be aware that their actions have an impact on other people—perhaps they are too busy thinking about other things or too busy thinking about themselves to realize the ripple effect they cause.

DEPENDABILITY

Remember, actions speak louder than words. Just as responsibility has two sides, so does dependability—being dependable to yourself and being dependable to those you are leading.

It is not complicated, do what you say you are going to do when you say you are going to do it.

Now I understand that life is fluid and things can change in an instant causing plans to be altered. This was discussed previously when the issue of respect was ad- dressed. But if as a leader other feel they cannot count on you; it will also make it difficult for you to count on them. When you are the leader of a group or activity, the others will mirror your behavior. If you are not taking the task seriously then the others will follow your actions and also not take it seriously. So, if you are not dependable, how can you hold others accountable? For example, a supervisor who is always late to work and takes long lunches will have trouble disciplining an employee for doing the same thing. Remember, as a leader the people around you are aware of your actions whether you realize it or not.

COMMITMENT

It is simple. If you say you are going to do something, do it. Once you make a commitment, keep it. When leading a team, you agree to put in the time or resources needed to lead the group down the path to success. If the leader gives up so will the rest of the team. So, don't give up before you reach the goal.

Cherokee Wisdom

There are a variety of commitments we make in our personal life. If we have credit cards, which most of us do, we make a commitment to the company to pay the debt in a timely manner. When a company hires us, we make a commitment to work for an exchange of money. In a marriage, we make a commitment to the other person to adhere to the vows. When we have children, we make a commitment to that child that we will be their caretaker until they reach adulthood.

Loyalty is a big part of commitment. If I am your friend and am loyal to you, I make a commitment that I will do my best to not hurt or harm you. Though not everyone keeps their commitments, we all have situations where we make them.

For example, many of us have had the experience of going on a diet with the intention of losing weight. After a few weeks, most give up only to be frustrated and then put on even more weight. Admittedly, it is not always easy to keep committed because there are so many distractions. Just turn on the TV and you see food commercials. We live in a society where eating out is a social event. We go to restaurants and coffee houses to socialize so that food becomes a bonding ritual.

Cherokee Wisdom

Of course, fad diets come and go. However, adopting a healthy lifestyle can help you in the long run. But if you feel like you are being deprived you may give up. So, it is important to find a sustainable weight management program. Not one that starves yourself or pressures you to get up at the crack of dawn and go to the gym. Using the buddy system can also help you stay accountable. The easy thing to do is to walk away when the going gets tough. The difficult thing can be staying until the goal is reached, and then recalibrating so that you can maintain your success. Keep in mind you should strive to be at a healthy weight for the right reasons. The best reason is your well-being. After all, if you are overweight it can affect all areas of your life. And, your health is not only important for yourself but also for the people who love you.

I know I have had my share of ups and downs with weight. At the end of the day I had to stop thinking about the situation and incorporate the idea of living a healthy lifestyle. Making good food choices and exercising on a regular basis have become part of my routine. Since I am not a fan of going to the gym, I walk, hike, dance and have a personal trainer who comes to my home three times per week. Doing these things, I enjoy helps me keep the commitment I made to myself to stay healthy.

Life happens, so learn to adjust. If you understand that life can be fluid and there will always be unexpected delays or challenges, you will be able to adapt. You can help yourself in this process by developing a plan and generally sticking to it even if you hit a brick wall. If you hit a brick wall adjust— can go over it, around it or through it. The end result is that others will know that you are a responsible person and when you are committed to something, you follow through.

When I think of leadership and commitment, I think of Ron Andrade who is the executive director of the Native American Indian Commission in Los Angeles. He has served in this position for many years. During his tenure, he has had to fight to keep the government funding for the commission, and he has had to deal with other political and community battles. He has had to rise above the differences and stay committed to the primary purpose of the commission, which is to increase the acquisition and application of resources to address the socioeconomic concerns of American Indians in Los Angeles City and County. He has never lost sight of this goal and has stayed committed to serving the Native American community. He is a member of the La Jolla Indian Reservation.

LEADERSHIP LESSON #10

As a leader be responsible, accountable and dependable to yourself and to your team. Commitment helps you stay on course until the job is finished and then stay diligent to maintain or build upon the level of success you achieved.

Wisdom from Abraham Bearpaw

>>>Responsible<<<

In times past Tribal people have always felt a sense of responsibility for others. This holds true today in Indigenous communities though it is not a value common to western society. However, with the current pandemic all Americans are starting to see how our actions can affect others. Right now, we are being asked to stay home in order to slow the

Cherokee Wisdom

rate of infection so that we do not overwhelm our medical resources. That's it. We can save our lives and the lives of others if we just stay home. However, many are refusing to heed this warning or listen to the advice of medical professionals. Now there are protests coming from segments of the population who are not willing to be responsible for others. However, while this is situation has prompted an unfortunate and inconsiderate reaction by some people, the majority of Americans are acting in a responsible manner.

Every day I see the majority of our countrymen show that they are willing to be responsible for themselves and others and it is inspiring. This pandemic has shown no preference or deference for anyone and this commonality now bonds us together but some more than most. People from very different backgrounds and socio-economic status all find themselves now linked by a new term; essential worker. While the rest of us are being asked to stay home these brave women and men put themselves in harm's way for their families and communities and we owe them all a debt of gratitude. If I show in my actions that I feel responsible for you and you for I then we will all succeed together.

Cherokee Wisdom

"I feel that not just Cherokee people but poor people in general have a much greater capacity for leadership and for solving their own problems than they're ever given credit for."

Wilma Mankiller
Cherokee Nation Principal
1985-1995

Cherokee Wisdom

Eleven: Patient

anvnidiyu

Be patient, no matter what you are going through.

We live in a society of instant gratification. We want things now. Many people, particularly the millennials, do not want to pay their dues for the top job. They want to start at the top. But for most people it does not work that way. As was discussed in previous chapters, it is important that you do not try to control everything and everyone around you. If they are not cooperating in the way you want, sometimes rather than using a stick, you need to be patient and let them figure things out on their own.

After all, it is their journey in life that is unfolding for them.

Cherokee Wisdom

So, patience is an awareness that things happen in God's time, not ours. However, the ego can get in the way and then we want things to happen when we want them to happen. Put your ego aside then and realize that there is a divine order and everything happens at the exact time it is meant to happen.

Personally, I am the type of person who likes to set goals and plan things. Once I develop a plan, I want to execute it and hope it goes according to design. When obstacles and challenges arise, I can get impatient. But once I practice patience and let the ego go, I can understand the reasons why things turned out the way they did.

One of the best examples of patience I can think of is the Sand Mandala, which is a Tibetan Buddhist tradition involving the creation and destruction of etchings made from colored sand. It takes many hours to create these beautiful masterpieces and a person's patience definitely helps them with the difficult task of completing such a meticulous project. It is singularly important to not focus on that fact that as soon as the mandala is finished it will be destroyed. But instead to focus on the task at hand. A sand mandala is ritualistically dismantled once it has been completed and the accompanying ceremonies and viewings symbolize the Buddhist doctrinal belief in the transitory nature of material life.

Your patience can definitely be tested when you are dealing directly with some people. One way to increase your patience with others is to work on acceptance and tolerance. As I wrote earlier, acceptance means you accept that other people are different from you, which goes hand in hand with them having their own ideas and thoughts. This does not mean you have to agree with them but starting with the idea that you accept them for who they are is one of the first steps toward learning patience.

Take a look at your own life and see which times you are impatient. Is it while waiting in line at the bank, stuck in traffic, trying to be understood by someone you are close with? When you react in a negative way, does that make the line move any faster? No, it only causes you to become more anxious, irritable or angry.

Most people who fly off the handle after becoming impatient usually have bigger problems. They may have unresolved issues that trigger their anger. Their anger may even be so deeply rooted that they may not be aware it is there. For example, people who experienced physical, sexual or mental abuse as a child can have unresolved feelings which surface in unexpected ways. For them, seeking professional help is often helpful to heal their wounds.

The other concept in having patience is, the realization that nothing lasts forever. Or said in another way, everything in life is temporary. If you are going through a dark period, find comfort in the fact it will not last forever. The light will shine again.

We have all felt pain, sorrow or uncertainty at some time in our life. The challenges we face in our lives are for a reason, usually to teach us a lesson. If you can practice patience, you will ultimately get through the rough spots.

Even when there is a powerful storm, after it is gone the sky is once again blue. During the storm it may be scary and difficult to imagine there will be another beautiful day, but just know there will be. I guarantee it.

There is also a difference between being patient and being passive. Just because you are a patient person does not mean you allow yourself to be mistreated or abused. Set boundaries and stand up for yourself if others are mistreating you.

When I think about the opposite of patience, I think about someone being anxious or angry. When someone is anxious it is usually because in their own mind, they are playing out all of the scenarios of what could happen. This does not mean they are going to happen; it is just what they worry could happen – as a point of fact, the majority of what people worry about never comes to pass.

Reflecting on my own life, there were times when I was forced to practice patience. I now understand even better doing so was for my greater good. I'll tell you a story. Several years ago, I was appointed to a political position. I was working hard and doing a good job. Due to circumstances beyond my control, I was suddenly removed from the role. At first, I was devastated and took it personally. Very quickly though I put my ego aside and regained and maintained my integrity, then practiced patience and took the high road. As time went by, I realized what had happened and it turned out to be a blessing. Actually, everything worked out in my favor. I am so glad I was able to step back, be patient and have faith.

Cherokee Wisdom

You may not get everything how and when you want it, but learning to "go with the flow" helps. Going with the flow used to seem counterintuitive to me. After all, I am the type of person who sets goals and makes plans. But going with the flow has taught me if plan A does not work then go to plan B. In fact, when you are the leader you realize there are times when you must have a plan B and a plan C.

If we all practiced more patience, the world would be a better place.

LEADERSHIP LESSON #11

A great leader exercises patience with him/herself and others. They know that challenges are temporary and the benefits come from focusing on the long haul.

Cherokee Wisdom

Wisdom from Abraham Bearpaw (Bear)

>>>Patient<<<

When I was newly sober in AA I was often told that if I continued to do my work then good things would happen but the time frame was "sometimes quickly, sometimes slowly". This was often shared with an unconscious shrug of the shoulders because the person relaying the message was totally unconcerned with my schedule or time frame. Being patient is a skill that I still work at every day and applies not just to my sobriety but all facets of my life. The weird thing to me is that the more patient that I become then the quicker that I achieve my goals in life.

Cherokees have a different concept of time and we believe that things happen when they are supposed to and will not necessarily occur on our time frame. In the business world we understand that deadlines must be met but we can be patient with our team members and ourselves throughout the course of our work. Our patience will allow ourselves and others to grow and learn and will lead to more productivity in the long run.

Cherokee Wisdom

"I don't think anybody anywhere can talk about the future of his or her people or of an organization without talking about education. Whoever controls the education of our children controls our future."

Wilma Mankiller
Cherokee Nation Principal
1985-1995

Twelve: Teacher
dideyohvsgi

Share your knowledge and wisdom with others to improve an individual, family or group.

I do not have all the answers. But if I can share the lessons I have learned from my ancestors and others along my journey to help make someone else's life become easier then I have accomplished a goal that is important to me.

When you get to the core of what teaching is, it is a sharing of information from one person to another. Though when I talk about teaching, most assume learning is taking place through formal education in a structured environment such as school, college or university. Yes, that is the way

Cherokee Wisdom

most of us learn. But when you really think about it, not only do we learn from the textbooks but we also learn from each other. For example, most of us remember someone who had an influence on our life such as a teacher, principal, neighbor, family, friend or coach.

When we are born, we essentially only have inbred knowledge from our genetics. We then learn how to walk, talk and behave. All the while, we acquire knowledge through our interaction with our family and those around us. And as we get older, we learn from our friends, co-workers, groups and even the media.

Our life is a process of learning. We gather external input through our senses. We hear, smell, taste and feel. We learn by reading, watching, talking, listening, feeling and touching.

So, as we become more mature, we can process information in different ways. Some people are visual learners, others auditory learners. There is not one way to learn and in fact since everyone is different, people learn in different ways.

In the Native American culture, we have Elders who teach us. These Elders share customs,

Cherokee Wisdom

traditions and stories. They are respected for their knowledge and are looked up to. They are the guiding lights of the tribe and as a part of having gained wisdom through their life experiences, they love to share their knowledge and pass it on to the next generation.

A great example of this is Wes Studi, who is a Cherokee actor. His work has been seen in many movies including Avatar, Dancing with Wolves and Geronimo to name a few. A few years ago, he collaborated with the Center for Disease Control to do a public service announcement (PSA) on the issue of type 2 diabetes.

Since the 1950's the diet of Native Americans has drastically changed and they are now consuming more processed food while at the same time becoming less active. As a result, type 2 diabetes has become a problem, one that did not exist before.

The message in the PSA was simple—return to the lifestyle of our ancestors. Eat healthy and be active. In the past, Cherokee meals revolved around what is referred to as the "Three Sisters" (corn, beans and squash) plus a protein like salmon. Garden fresh vegetables and fruits were included

Cherokee Wisdom

in the meals. An active lifestyle and plenty of water was also part of the daily routine. Making good choices helped maintain a balance, which is what Cherokees strived for in their lives. The message Wes is trying to convey is for the greater good of the people. He is trying to teach the younger generation about the past so they can better control this disease. Though there is no cure it can be managed.

When you are the leader you share your knowledge and expertise with others so they can be empowered. As each person within the group acquires new skills it will help the entire group grow stronger. In short, when all members of a group are empowered, they have a better chance of reaching the collective goal.

Some leaders are hesitant to share their wisdom because they are insecure or ignorant. Somehow, they believe if the group is empowered, they will become irrelevant. I have found the opposite to be true. When I have shared my knowledge with those I was working with, they became stronger and worked better as a team.

Cherokee Wisdom

As a leader it is important to recognize that each team member is starting with a different skill set. Some team members may need your attention more than others. This may require you to perform an individual skills analysis at the start of the project to assess the team. Then work with each person based on his or her ability. As a leader, the team is counting on you to assist them in accomplishing the goals. Ideally, teaching comes from a place of caring and compassion. What does that mean? The person doing the teaching should share their wisdom to benefit other people, and not try and control them.

In today's society some of the students do not have respect for the teachers. That discord is compounded by our educational system being in need of significant improvements. One area of concern is that teachers' pay is not consistent with how important their job is—they are shaping the next generation and should be compensated accordingly. Another serious area of concern is our schools have in some cases become a breeding ground for violence and negativity. It is hard for the students to learn if they do not feel safe, just as it is challenging to teach if the environment is not conducive to learning.

Cherokee Wisdom

If as a society we want to develop the next generation of dynamic leaders, we must invest in our educational system. For example, colleges and universities should be affordable and accessible for the entire population. In other countries around the world there is a greater emphasis on education as a long-term investment for society.

Just as we all have the ability to be a great leader, we all have the ability to share our knowledge and be teachers. So, take it upon yourself to help the next generation.

As you progress through the stages of life, turn around and help the generation behind you. Be a mentor, tutor or just a friend. There are many young people that can use a positive role model. Share the lessons which you have learned in this book and help them along their path.

LEADERSHIP LESSON #12

A leader should share their knowledge for the benefit of others and for the overall successful achievement of goals.

Cherokee Wisdom

Words from Abraham Bearpaw

>>>Teacher<<<

Perhaps the most important thing we contribute in life is the example that we set for others. To teach others how to live in a good way and walk in balance. As Cynthia Ruiz has pointed out, everyone is a teacher because others are always watching what you do. Though you may not be aware of it there is always someone watching what you do and may be looking to you for guidance. On several occasions, others have commented on how my actions influenced them rather than my words.

So, while it is important for you to say good things, I believe it is your actions that will teach others the most about your values.

The best leaders are willing to teach others how to be leaders themselves and that is sorely needed in the world today. I would be very happy for this to be my legacy one day. That I was able to teach others how to walk in balance and lead others. This is the main reason for me to write these words.

Cherokee Wisdom

Historically, Natives have mostly passed on our values orally to the next generation but I want it recorded that I struggled and persevered because others cared to teach me. Then when I learned these values and lessons, I cared enough to help others and on it will go for eternity. That circle can never be broken if we are willing to learn from others and then teach what we learned. Remember that it is never too late to be who you might have been.

Wado Cynthia Ruiz for your leadership and for the opportunity to be of service. Also, I say wado to all of you who are leading by example during these trying times.

Cherokee Wisdom

"The Cherokee legacy is that we are a people who face adversity, survive, adapt, prosper and excel."

Chad Smith
Principal Chief of the Cherokee Nation
1999-2011

Cherokee Wisdom

Our Ancestors
kanohesginulistanv

History of the Cherokee people

Let me start by saying that we are not history experts, however, we feel it is important to share some of the amazing histories of our people. Sharing this information is our way of hoping that this information continues on and that others learn from it. We hope this gives you an understanding of how brave and courageous the Cherokee people

Cherokee Wisdom

are and how blessed we are to have come from an amazing tribe. The information in this section came from several sources including but not limited to stories passed down from the ancestors, Cherokee Nation, and the Cherokee Heritage Center.

Since there was no written Cherokee language until 1821, what we know about the beginning history and early stages of the tribe was passed from down through storytelling. Storytelling is a very important part of the Cherokee culture and history.

According to Cherokee Nation, the first recorded encounters with the Europeans were with Spanish explorer Hernando DeSoto in 1540. DeSoto and his conquistadors were on an expedition seeking gold which took them across much of the "new world," including trekking through what is now Florida, Georgia, the Carolinas, Tennessee, Alabama, Arkansas, and Mississippi.

The Cherokee people were hit hard by disease brought over by the Europeans including smallpox. In 1738 it was estimated that 50% of the Cherokee population died from the smallpox epidemic.

Cherokee Wisdom

The Cherokee people are made up of three tribes:

1 Cherokee Nation in Tahlequah
2 Keetoowah Band of Cherokee
3 Eastern Band in North Carolina

The Cherokee Nation of Oklahoma, which we are a part of, was officially established on September 6, 1839, but obviously, the tribe existed long before then. There is no written documentation when the tribe may have come into existence, but it is safe to say they were the first inhabitants of this land before the Europeans colonized it.

The Cherokee Tribe was divided into seven clans or families. The Cherokee society is matrilineal meaning the clan line is traced through the mother.

The seven clans are:

1 Long hair
2 Paint
3 Bird

Cherokee Wisdom

4   Wolf

5   Wild Potato

6   Deer

7   Blue

Since the clans were considered families, marriage between clan members was not permitted.

Each clan had a representative at the general council, the white council during peaceful times and a red council during war times. In 1753 a Grand Council was developed which evolved into a National Council.

The primary belief of the Cherokee people was that the world should be in balance. If something was out of balance then it should be corrected. There was a rule called blood law (clan law), if one person killed a person from another clan (even if accidental) then to correct the balance the clan which lost a member could take the life of the other clan to restore balance.

A state of "wellness" is described as "harmony between the mind, body, and spirit." The Cherokee word "tohi" - health - is the same as the word for peace. You're in good health when your body is at peace. Also, the "medicine circle" has no beginning and no end and therefore represents a concept of "harmonious unity."

The Cherokee people were hunters, gatherers, and farmers. Before the mid-eighteenth century, women did most of the farming while men were responsible for hunting, fishing, and clearing fields for planting. Women also owned the farms, homes, and most possessions, except for hunting weapons.

The basic food of the Cherokee is what is referred to as the "Three Sisters": corn, beans, and squash. Turkey, deer, fish roots, potatoes, and pumpkin were also part of their meals. So basically, they lived off the land from what they were able to gather or hunt.

The Cherokee originally wore clothing made from animal skins before the Europeans introduced woven cloth to the tribe. Even into the 1800s, the men wore leggings made of deer hide to protect their legs from thorns and underbrush. A beaded belt was also worn around the waist.

The Cherokee never wore headdresses. Warriors usually shaved or plucked their heads except for a

Cherokee Wisdom

single scalp- lock towards the back of the head; they would then tie to it one eagle or turkey feather. Later, the men wore woven turbans made of hide or cloth. Sequoyah is always pictured wearing a turban. Both men and women wore moccasins.

Music was also a big part of the culture and they played such instruments as the water drum, river cane flute, and trumpets. Turtle shells were used as ceremonial rattles.

Stickball was a game that was established for conflict resolution and was known as the game of little war. In later years it became a social game and women were allowed to play.

Ceremony was a significant part of the culture as well. Normally participants who were making a religious commitment to the ceremony would take medicine for their physical and spiritual benefit. This medicine was made from roots and plants which had been gathered by the "medicine helpers" and prepared by the Heles Haya (medicine man).

One of the most significant ceremonies was popularly known as the Stomp Dance, which contained both religious and social meaning. The term "Stomp Dance" is of English origin and refers

Cherokee Wisdom

to the "shuffle and stomp" movements of the dance. It remains highly significant to this day. Both men and women participated and the line was one man than a woman back to a man etc.

To the Cherokees, the Stomp Dance has always been affiliated with the Green Corn Ceremony.

During the Green Corn Ceremony as practiced by the Cherokees, one of the two social dances performed is ancient and originated from the mother city of Keetoowah. The dance is called ye-lu-le, which means "to the center." During this dance, all of the dancers' shout "ye-lu-le" and move towards the fire in the center of the sacred dance circle. The dance symbolizes the dispersal of the sacred fire given to the Keetoowah people by the Creator.

As in most native cultures, the four directions were honored and recognized.

They prayed in the four cardinal directions:

1. East
2. North
3. West
4. South

Cherokee Wisdom

Also, the Cherokees recognized three more directions:

5 Up (above)
6 Down (below)
7 Center (where you are)

Not all tribes honored the seven directions, however, the Cherokee people had a three-dimensional view of the world and prayed in seven directions. During ceremonies plants were used to clear the energy, specifically, sweetgrass and cedar were used since it was readily available in the area.

CHEROKEE SYLLABARY

In 1821 Sequoyah completed the creation of a Cherokee syllabary, a system of 6 characters, making reading and writing in Cherokee possible. It had taken then 12 years to develop the syllabary. He first introduced it to his daughter and then once she learned it, he was able to teach to others. The Cherokees were the first Tribe to have their own educational system.

Cherokee Wisdom

Trail of Tears
The Cherokee Removal

In 1829, when gold was discovered in Georgia, everything changed for the tribe. In 1830 Congress passed the Relocation Act. Cherokees were forcibly removed from their homeland by Federal Troops and had to relocate 1,000 miles, marching until they reached Oklahoma.

An estimated 4,000 died from hunger, exposure, and disease in the internment camps along the trail itself as well as after their arrival due to the effects of the journey. This became what is known today as the Trail of Tears. It took over four months to travel the long distance in very harsh conditions.

Since that time Tahlequah, Oklahoma became the center of the Cherokee Nation and operates now under a three-part government including judicial, executive, and legislative branches.

Dawes Roll

The Dawes Act of February 8, 1887, developed an inventory of the Native people in that area. A

Cherokee Wisdom

federal commission tasked with creating Final Rolls for the Cherokees, Chickasaws, Choctaws, Creeks, and Seminoles in Indian Territory (present-day Oklahoma). Oklahoma did not become a State until 1907. In 1989 there were 39 different tribes in Oklahoma. Today the Dawes Roll is used to establish tribal membership.

Today

There are almost 600 federally-recognized Indian tribes in the United States today, each with their individual history. Cherokee Nation is the largest Tribe.

The Cherokee Nation is a thriving community with over 370,000 citizens. The Cherokee Nation is a sovereign tribal government. Cherokee Business manages a prosperous gaming portfolio that funds schools, hospitals, and services for the community. Cherokee Nation employs just over 11,000 employees many are tribal citizens.

The citizens elect their representatives and Principal Chief.

Cherokee Wisdom

Cherokee National Holiday

The tradition continues today with the Cherokee National Holiday, which is celebrated each year at the beginning of September during Labor Day Weekend. The holiday has been observed annually since 1953 to commemorate the signing of the 1839 Cherokee Constitution and attracts nearly 100,000 visitors from around the world. The celebration includes a powwow, which is one of the largest powwows in the United States. Many events are held and the Principal Chief gives the annual State of the Nation Speech. This multi-day celebration is jam-packed with sports activities for all ages, from traditional games such as Cherokee marbles, the cornstalk shoot, and blowgun competition to the more familiar golf and softball tournaments. The celebration includes a powwow, which is one of the largest powwows in the United States.

Our history lives on through the Cherokee Heritage Center, which keeps valuable records of the Cherokee people and makes them available to the public. The records in their collection trace the events and decisions that shaped the Cherokee

Cherokee Wisdom

Nation. The center also has a village so visitors can see how life was for the Cherokee People. The village has a large stickball arena where traditional games are played.

For more information visit the Cherokee Nation's web site:
    www.cherokee.org

Cherokee Heritage Center's website:
    www.cherokeeheritage.org

Recommended reading:

Cherokee Nation recommends A History of Survival, Self Determination, and Identity 1/ 1/ 2018 by Dr. Bob Blackburn, Dr. Duane King and, Dr. Neil Morton

Cherokee Wisdom

Cherokee Holiday 2019

Jesse Ruiz, Gina Olaya, Cynthia Ruiz, Felicia Olaya,
Sister Weeping Willow & Abraham Bearpaw
left to right

In closing I would like say how grateful I am to you for your time and attention. I would like to share a prayer I wrote a few years ago. This was written while taking a prayer class at the AGAPE International Spiritual Center in Los Angeles.

Our class assignment was to write our own prayer. At first, I questioned myself and thought, who am I to write a prayer? Then I realized why not since this is my way of communicating with the Creator. Just like with leadership, we all have the innate ability for thoughtful prayer.

Cherokee Wisdom

Gratitude to the Creator by Lion Mother

Creator, Great Spirit who I call God.
I humbly stand before you, to praise you.
For you are I…. and. I am you.
I welcome you into my heart, body and soul.

Grant me the wisdom to follow my inner voice,
The strength to stay grounded while I sing my scared song.

Guide me down my chosen path with the courage to pursue
what is available to me.

Allow me to receive the infinite possibilities of the universe.
I am appreciative for my lessons yet grateful for the struggles.

I am comforted by the wonderful people you
have placed in my life.

Cherokee Wisdom

Creator, Great Spirit who I call God.
I walk with the strength and humility of my ancestors.
I honor Mother Earth for the gifts she provides.
The fertile soil provides our daily food and the gift of water is the essence of life.

Open my heart to the healing of mother nature.
We are all connected and through this I find serenity.
May I never stop being a beneficial presence on this planet.

Work through me to carry the message of peace and unconditional love.

Guide me to bring harmony and balance into this world.
I am complete having you in my life.
Creator, Great Spirit who I call God.

Made in United States
Troutdale, OR
06/15/2025